SCOTLAND'S WAR

SEONA ROBERTSON
AND LES WILSON

MAINSTREAM
PUBLISHING

EDINBURGH AND LONDON

Dedicated to Ian Robertson and Harry Wilson, warriors of Bomber Command, and to Muriel and Gladys, the women they came home to.

Copyright © Seona Robertson and Leslie Wilson, 1995

First published in Great Britain in 1995 by
MAINSTREAM PUBLISHING COMPANY (EDINBURGH) LTD
7 Albany Street
Edinburgh EH1 3UG

ISBN 1 85158 700 4

A catalogue record for this book is available from the British Library

Designed by Janene Reid

Printed and bound in Great Britain by Butler & Tanner Ltd, Frome

PREVIOUS PAGE: 'Pretty good shooting' – ATS women on the night barrage
(Imperial War Museum)

CONTENTS

ACKNOWLEDGMENTS

4

This book would not have been possible without the commitment of Gus Macdonald of Scottish Television, who let us embark on a five-year project when he did not have a broadcasting franchise to complete it. Alistair Moffat initiated the idea and was succeeded by David Scott, Blair Jenkins and Maxine Baker, all enthusiastic executive producers. It was Maxine who finally encouraged us to write the book. And, when writing the text, it was impossible not to hear the marvellous voice of our narrator, Tom Watson.

Film crews and production staff – too numerous to mention by name – brought their skills and a genuine involvement to *Scotland's War*. We must single out a few production people, such as dubbing mixer Brian Paterson and editors Andy Boyd and Peter Blackie for their dedication to duty. Alf Penn's encyclopaedic knowledge of archive film was invaluable to the series and he has performed miracles of photograph research for this book. In his research for interviews and archive material, Ken Neil – our 'adjutant' during four of the five years we all 'lived' this war – was meticulous, dedicated and creative.

We have had invaluable help from many archives and museums. All the staff of the film and photographic departments of the Imperial War Museum, especially Paul Sergeant and Jane Fish, have been unfailingly helpful and enthusiastic. Exiled Scot Larry McKinna of British Pathé News as well as the staff at British Movietone News hunted for rare Scottish items. Janet McBain of the Scottish Film Archive, Stephen Wood of the Scottish United Services Museum and Ann Marwick of Historic Scotland in Orkney put us on the track of many interesting stories. Numerous regimental and services associations and museums assisted with research and guided us to interviewees.

We gratefully acknowledge permission to reproduce M-O material from the Trustees of the Tom Harrisson Mass-Observation Archive; an extract from Crown copyright British Cabinet Records CAB 66/3 from the Controller of Her Majesty's Stationery Office; Noel Coward lyrics from Chappell Music Ltd and International Music Publications Ltd; 'Don't Sit Under the Apple Tree' (Brown, Tobias, Stept) lyrics from EMI, Redwood Music Ltd and the Concord Partnership; extracts from the Churchill, Rommel and Johnston memoirs from the Churchill estate and Collins; and photographs from the public collections and individuals credited in the captions.

Jeremy Isaacs gave us practical support on this series and his own achievement in demonstrating the lasting value of television history is a constant inspiration. Bill Campbell and his colleagues at Mainstream Publishing, Judy Diamond and Richard Mellis in editorial and Janene Reid in design, remained calm under fire as our deadline was shot to pieces and were immensely supportive of the project.

Aileen Kane, our partner in Caledonia, Sterne & Wyld, our independent production company, suffered along with us as we tried to distil all this history. She brought an objective eye as well as a lot of hard work to the venture.

Above all, we wish to thank all the men and women without whose testimony the television series, this book and the unique archive *Scotland's War* has become, would not exist.

FOREWORD

Scotland's War was the most ambitious documentary series ever made in Scotland. It was certainly the longest, comprising thirty episodes spread over five years.

The first episode was screened on 3 September 1989 to coincide with the fiftieth anniversary of the start of the Second World War. The series proved popular with viewers and critics alike.

No experts took part – *Scotland's War* was based on the experiences of ordinary people who lived through some of the most turbulent events of this century. The series therefore created a uniquely valuable archive of eye-witness reaction to one of the most frightening and tumultuous periods of the twentieth century. This book adds to what is already an important piece of Scottish social history

Gus Macdonald,
Managing Director,
Scottish Television

Churchill and pipers of the 51st Highland Division, Germany, March 1945 (Imperial War Museum)

INTRODUCTION

Sharing the memories of more than three hundred members of Scotland's Second World War generation was an extraordinary experience. Here was a virtually untapped source of Scottish history. As well as a valuable addition to the history of a small nation, it was an insight into a world-wide conflict that shaped every one of our lives today.

Interviews were the backbone of *Scotland's War*, a popular and much praised television documentary series. People from all walks of life – and in all of Scotland's dialects – told us of their lives between 1939 and 1945. Personal photographs were extracted from wallets, or rediscovered in drawers and attics. We had used transcripts to edit the programmes and it soon became obvious that what we'd recorded was as gripping on the printed page as on the screen. The idea of this book was born.

Our parents' generation – servicepeople and civilians, men and women, Highlanders and Lowlanders – poured out their stories for us. Under the glare of the lights, our camera recorded over two hundred hours of vivid recollection. Much of it had been bottled up for years. A merchant seaman, veteran of the Arctic convoys, was brought to the interview by his son, who told us afterwards that his father had never talked of many of these experiences. Normally reticent people – ex-prisoners of the Japanese, for instance – told their harrowing tales to 'outsiders' for the first time in their lives. Were they beginning to realise that their 'typical' experiences were in fact history? Was it that a generation – increasingly losing contemporaries through natural causes – was being reminded of those it had lost in Normandy, Burma, Clydebank, the Atlantic and the skies above Berlin?

That generation seemed to have decided to put its collective memory on record. We were privileged to listen. Much of what they told us could not be squeezed into the series, and even less into this book. We made thousands of agonising choices. The Imperial War Museum's offer to house the entire unedited collection of video interviews has come as a great relief to us. Now there is the possibility of historians and programme-makers of the future using these memories again and making different choices.

In *Scotland's War* we have examined combat by concentrating on the experiences of one or two Scottish formations in a particular campaign, rather than attempting an overview. And so, there is much about Scottish regiments and the Merchant Navy while there is little about the Scottish contribution to the mixed crews of the RAF. However, there is resonance in describing an action through the varied views of a group of friends who survived it together. The first such chapter, 'Left in France' tells of the surrender of the 51st Highland Division at Saint Valery in 1940, mainly through the eyes of Cameron Highlanders from the Uists and Royal Artillerymen from Millport. Our concentration on 'Scottishness' allowed us to look at stories too personal or 'untidy' to fit into the general sweep of history. Jeremy Isaacs, who we approached for an interview about being evacuated as a child, encouraged us to tackle the Highland Division's fate which never found a place in his series *The World at War*.

Much of *Scotland's War* is not actually concerned with war. While there was an unrepeatable intensity in life at the battle front, many Scots on the home front remember profound, often life-changing experiences. Recalling the terrible suffering of servicemen and blitzed civilians, some almost apologise when describing their 'good war'. Many women were away from the home in the forces, perhaps seeing the world, entering the factory or Land Army – taking on jobs 'women can't do'. The war was also an opportunity to form all kinds of friendships and unexpected romances and to meet the foreigners who flooded into Scotland. American GIs, Jewish refugees, Polish and French forces in exile, English and Commonwealth troops training in the Highlands, and German and Italian war brides and prisoners-of-war all played their part in *Scotland's War* – and changed us a little, forever.

Have memories of the good times blotted out the bad, as one ATS girl thought? Recollections of the communal, supportive nature of the last war – living life to the full, often right on the edge, suffering hardship together with fewer class barriers – have perhaps blunted feelings of greyness, fear, boredom, despair or loss. Perhaps that is a comment on youth versus age, or on our own times. And yet again some are not nostalgic. One woman said, 'We survived. But I wouldn't like to go through it again.'

This volume is not the definitive history of Scotland's experience of the Second World War – it is simply an account of what it felt like, told through the experiences and in the words of some who were there. Errors and omissions are ours. The credit is all theirs.

CHAPTER 1

The Balloon Goes Up

I can remember it was 3 September 1939. It was a Sunday morning about nine o'clock. I remember my father coming in and he kissed me on the forehead and said: 'Well, son, that's me away to the sodgers.' I never saw him again for two and a half years.

Tommy McSorley, Glasgow

Two days after German bombers raided shipping in the Forth – the first air-raid on Britain – barrage balloons were flown from ships on the river, 18 October 1939 (603 Squadron Archives)

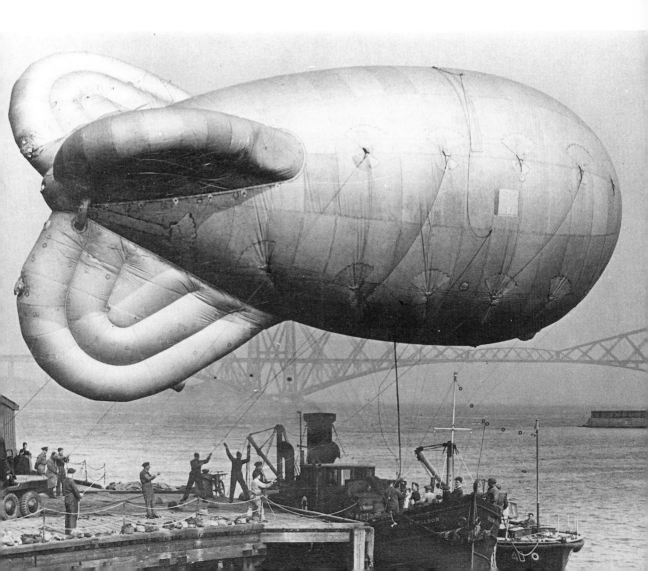

We knew that Hitler was evil and we knew that fascism had to be destroyed. But it was with mixed feelings that you looked at your brother and thought, he is the one who is going to have to go and fight.

Bella Keyzer, Dundee

The war came early to Scotland. While the rest of the UK played at national emergency in the 'Bore' War until the Spitfire Summer of 1940, the Scots discovered that the Nazis meant business. When war was declared, the SS *Athenia* was on its way from the Clyde to Canada.

The liner, with about 1,400 people aboard including over 1,000 passengers, was out-ward bound across the Atlantic – virtually a refugee ship – when, without any warning whatsoever, she was torpedoed by a Nazi submarine 200 miles west of the Hebrides.

The Crime of the Athenia, **British Movietone News, September 1939**

The word had gone round to abandon ship, from the Master on the bridge. Our job was to get the lifeboats down to the embarkation deck, get the passengers aboard and lower them into the water. Unfortunately the boat I was in got into difficulties when we got alongside the rescue boat. The lifeboat was sucked into the propeller and the officer gave the command for everybody to jump off. I jumped myself afterwards, otherwise I would have been cut in two. I started to get everybody round about the lifeboat to hang on to the grab line and I managed to get some of them up on to the keel. Unfortunately, as time wore on, some of them slipped away. They just couldn't hang on any longer. The weather was so severely cold and they were getting stiff and cold and they just let go . . .

Harry Dillon, Quartermaster, *Athenia*, Glasgow

This struck us very hard in the *Daily Record* office. Not at our morale, but it brought home the realisation that we were going to get this sort of story for the duration. I remember some people being terribly upset. One or two girls came into my office and just sat and cried. They had been down to see the survivors coming in.

Alastair Dunnett, journalist, Edinburgh

In the following months, Scotland was to score other sad firsts. On 14 October, a German U-Boat penetrated the safe harbour of Scapa Flow in Orkney to sink the battleship *Royal Oak*, with the loss of more than 800 lives.

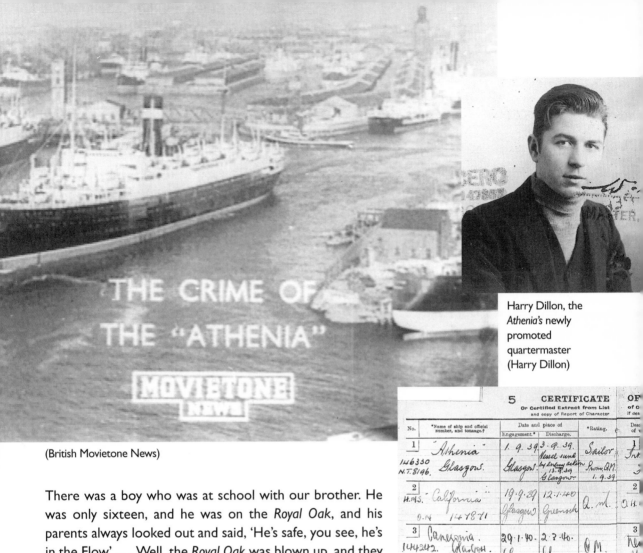

THE CRIME OF
THE "ATHENIA"

MOVIETONE
NEWS

(British Movietone News)

Harry Dillon, the
Athenia's newly
promoted
quartermaster
(Harry Dillon)

No.	*Name of ship and official number, and tonnage.†	Date and place of Engagement*	Discharge.†	*Rating.	Desc of
1	"Athenia" 146350 N.T. 8196. Glasgow.	1.9.39 Glasgow	3.9.39. Vessel sunk by enemy action 15.9.39 Glasgow	Sailor Prom.Q.M. 1.9.39	Int.
2	H.M.S. California O.N 147871	19.9.39 Glasgow	12.1.40 Greenock	Q.M.	O.H.
3	Cameronia 144242. Glasgow. 9606.	29.1.40. Glasgow	2.3.40. Glasgow	Q.M.	
4	CAMERONIA				

There was a boy who was at school with our brother. He was only sixteen, and he was on the *Royal Oak*, and his parents always looked out and said, 'He's safe, you see, he's in the Flow' ... Well, the *Royal Oak* was blown up, and they went to see what had happened. They went to the hospital in Kirkwall, and there was a boy there with the same name, but he wasn't theirs. That brought home almost immediately just what the war meant.

Joyce Anderson, Orkney

Within two days, a Renfrewshire farmer, a member of 602 City of Glasgow Auxiliary Fighter Squadron, shot down the first German plane over Britain.

Working on my farm, I used to see aeroplanes flying around and pilots being taught to fly. It interested me, so I went along and found that the Scottish Flying Club could teach me to fly at a cost of two pounds per hour. I applied to 602 and was granted a commission in 1933. The Auxiliary Air Force was really the same as the Territorial Army. The officers and the airmen were recruited from Glasgow. Among the officers

602 (City of Glasgow) Squadron's Hawker Harts on a pre-war exercise over Loch Lomond (George Pinkerton)

were bank clerks, stockbrokers, a plasterer, a miner and a couple of lawyers. The airmen came from all walks of life, many of them out of engineering works and technical jobs in the city. When it got really serious we were mobilised on 24 August. We were put on a war footing and we armed the aeroplanes and manned them. Of course we were proud of our ability to operate and we didn't really think the regulars had anything on us at all.

George Pinkerton, Houston

On 16 October German bombers raided shipping on the Forth estuary. Scotland's two fighter squadrons – 602 Glasgow and 603 Edinburgh – were scrambled to fight the first successful action in British skies.

We got fleeting glimpses of him but not sufficient to be able to fire at him. And when we got to the edge of a bank of cloud, he emerged – with me sitting on his starboard side and my number two sitting on his port side. We came up astern of him and carried out an attack. His aeroplane lifted up in the air and then went down into a dive and I think I had probably injured him in some way. My number two came in and gave him some more, and then I came back to finish him off. We watched how he flew over a merchant ship and then crashed down in the sea about a mile away. We were quite glad to see him in the sea because the last thing I wanted was to go back to my unit and say I hadn't shot him down! – considering that I had eight machine-guns that could fire ammunition at the rate of 2,400 rounds a minute.

George Pinkerton

I was quite excited and I said, 'I have just seen a German aeroplane being shot down.' 'Oh rubbish, it would be a practice do,' everyone said, even my dad at five o'clock at tea-time when he came in and I told him. Nobody would believe me!

Jim Lannan, Edinburgh

Pohle [the German pilot who had been shot down] had injured his face when his aeroplane hit the sea and he was taken to a hospital, a naval hospital at Port Edgar, and I went to see him there a few days later. After I went back home, I sent him some sweets and cigarettes and he wrote a letter thanking me.

George Pinkerton

George Pinkerton on the nose cone of his Spitfire
(George Pinkerton)

I thank you for the friendly conduct, wish you the best and greet with you likewise, the other pilot. To all airmen, comradeship. Helmut C.W. Pohle, Hauptmann der Luftwaffe.

Letter from Helmut Pohle to George Pinkerton

I don't think we thought of bombing. That perhaps came as a bit of a surprise when we discovered German aircraft could come this distance. And the first air-raids we had here . . . well, I was young and I found them quite exciting to tell the truth. I've no doubt that older people with more sense of what was happening didn't take that view. But we tended to look and watch and then discover what damage had been done. And the fact that we were being singled out . . . maybe there was a bit of pride about that.

Ian MacInnes, Orkney

Five months later, on 16 March 1940, the first British civilian was killed in an air-raid. Orkney, with its huge naval base and safe harbour at Scapa Flow, was a target for enemy bombers. German planes attacked the tiny hamlet of Brig of Waithe.

Well, the planes came over in the evening and I think they were probably dropping their bombs before they went. Four bombs fell round one house but the woman came out of that alive. I think it was the second lot of bombs, probably, that killed Jim Isbister. He was going out to help his neighbour who had been in the house that the four bombs had dropped on and he was killed in the doorway. He was just married lately with a wife and a small son.

Peter Leith, Isbister's cousin, Orkney

(Tankerness House
Museum, Orkney)

James Isbister's death was shocking national news but has now been largely forgotten by history, overshadowed by the city blitzes.

CHAPTER 2

The Guests of War

The sirens went off and it was really comical. Everybody was running about knocking each other over because you didn't know what to do. We had no shelters. We were all huddled in here thinking that we were going to get killed right away. It is funny looking back but of course it wasn't funny at the time.

Frieda Anderson, Edinburgh

When you hear these warning sirens take cover at once. The warning may also be given by short blasts on police whistles. The hand-rattle means gas. Put on your gas mask . . . and keep it on!

***Do it Now!*, Government information film, September 1939**

The fear of bombing caused the immediate evacuation of children (and, in Scotland, mothers and babies) from the big cities to the countryside.

They imagined they were just going to bomb Glasgow straight away and I can remember that Sunday; we all had little labels round our necks and gas-masks and we walked down to Kelvinbridge Station and were put on a train.

Betty Pearson, Glasgow

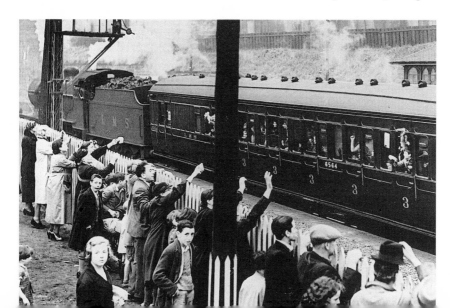

A train-load of
evacuees leaves
Glasgow on Sunday,
3 September 1939
(*Herald/Times*)

What I'll never forget was not so much the scene at Kelvinbridge Station or looking out of the window of the train, but the realisation that came to me just inside the front door of the flat in Hillhead, that my mother and father weren't coming too. I hadn't understood that and it was a wrench, but there wasn't time to do more than give them a kiss and off we went.

Jeremy Isaacs, Glasgow

We thought we were at the start of a great adventure. Everything was magic. When the train left you could hear the cheers. Half an hour later, out of the window, all I could see were these white things. The place was full of them. I was terrified in case these white animals should all gang up on us and eventually attack the whole train. It was only later on that I actually discovered they were sheep.

Tommy McSorley, Glasgow

When they came we were full of goodwill, and we thought, 'Oh, the poor dears coming from the towns will be so pleased to come to this beautiful country place.' Everybody was prepared to be kind to them. But one lady was very irate at being given children who were obviously verminous and took them to the local poorhouse to be deloused before she would take them home.

Helen Jackson, Perth

Resulting from the Government's evacuation of children, the City and County of Perth received many thousands of mothers, children of school age and pre-school children from Glasgow. From practically all districts, complaints have been received concerning the verminous and filthy condition of the children. In addition, many children were found to be suffering from infectious diseases such as diphtheria, impetigo, scabies and scarlet fever.

Perthshire Advertiser, **20 September 1939**

And then of course people lost their beds, and their mattresses, and so the goodwill began to evaporate. They weren't toilet-trained and the sanitation in some of the houses was a hut down the garden path, and the children wouldn't bother going there. They relieved themselves where they could. And that led to friction, as you can understand.

Helen Jackson

Walter Gordon's family in the comfortable suburb of Whitecraigs in the south of Glasgow took in evacuees from districts more vulnerable to bombing in Clydeside.

A WVS lady came and asked if we could take a family of three. As she was leaving she said to my father, 'You had better lift the carpet.' He was quite taken aback at this. 'Surely I don't need to lift the carpet?' And the WVS lady said, 'Well, the people who are coming will not have had carpets.' So it was with some apprehension that we awaited the arrival of this family. We had led a fairly protected kind of existence, but you don't really know that until you meet up with someone from another world, in a way. Only a few miles away, but another world.

Walter Gordon, Glasgow

The group of kids had been so neglected and filthy that they just stripped the clothes off them and had a great, hot bath ready. But this wee lad wasn't going into that bath and he screamed and yelled some incoherent phrase over and over again, and spread his arms and legs and they couldn't get him into the bath. Lady Elgin asked the housekeeper 'What is he saying?' The housekeeper replied, 'He's saying it's ower effin' deep and it's ower effin' hot.'

Alastair Dunnett, Edinburgh

My mother thought we had better give them a hot meal and I think she had mince or stew ready. The family couldn't really cope with that. My mother asked what they would eat and their mother said, 'Bread and jam.' We realised we were in the world of jeely pieces.

Walter Gordon

There were no chip shops. There was no cinema. They were appalled at what they found in the country, and they thought that we were primitive. And we thought that they were . . . oh dear! It was a complete clash of cultures.

Helen Jackson

We watched her milk this cow and the lady that owned the farm said, 'Would you like some?' I said 'No, there is no way I am going to drink that stuff. Cow's urine! I couldn't possibly drink that.' Milk came in bottles and was delivered to your doorstep.

Tommy McSorley

When our parents came down they couldn't understand a word we spoke. We spoke a broad Kirkcudbrightshire: 'hinnae ony and I dinna ken' and it was all very strange. So they were quite glad in the end when evacuation ended and we came back to Glasgow.

Jeremy Isaacs

OPPOSITE:
Evacuees leave Glasgow
(*Herald/Times*)

One set of Glasgow teenagers stayed on in Kirkcudbrightshire to complete their education.

Wartime PT – complete with gas masks! – for Glasgow evacuees at Cally House School, Gatehouse of Fleet
(Cally House School Former Pupils)

Today Cally House is no longer a celebrated private mansion. In September 1939, when the Government decided to evacuate schoolchildren from the big cities, they turned it into a co-educational boarding-school for 200 Glasgow secondary-school children.

Cally House, **archive film, 1942**

I had been an only child, happy, and suddenly – whoomph! One hundred brothers, one hundred sisters! That was good news to me. Sorry to leave my parents who might be bombed in Glasgow and all that, but I still had two hundred brothers and sisters. Great news.

John Campbell Bennet, Glasgow

We certainly missed the comforts of home because there were no carpets on the floor. Fires were few and far between and on cold days the only way of keeping yourself warm was to sit in bed with a hot-water bottle, filled from the tap. It depended on what you could get from the tap.

Edith Campbell, Glasgow

LEFT: The makeshift science lab at Cally House School (Cally House School Former Pupils)

RIGHT: Swimming at Sandgreen: the outdoor life for city girls (Cally House School Former Pupils)

We had fun, but we did work. We probably worked harder than we would have done at home because we had two hours' prep every night. That was a discipline and I have no doubt the staff were very keen to justify the whole thing. It was a big step for them and they were the ones who made it go.

Iain Cameron, Helensburgh

I think the outdoor life is what I remember best about being there. Going down to Sandgreen swimming – and I liked the gardening, believe it or not, doing the vegetables and going out to fields and hoeing the turnips. In the autumn we went out to the hedges on our bikes, and we collected brambles and made jam.

Joyce Christie, Edinburgh

Very few didn't go to the Saturday night dance. That meant dressing up and helping one another to share what clothes we had and gossiping about who was giving you the last waltz. That was very nice.

Jean Lowther, Edinburgh

Friendships were 'accommodated', shall we say, by the Saturday evening dances. Friendships of one kind or another!

Dr Tony Lowther, Edinburgh

I tell you one thing – we were told to go out in fours and not in twos because the normal connotation of this was that if you were out in twos, you were up to no good.

Iain Cameron

On sunny summer afternoons, you were able to wander off with the person of your choice, and find a bluebell glade and sit there and read poetry. That was the theory, anyway! I think it is fair to say that there was never anything that you might describe as 'trouble'. At least that's what we firmly believe. That's our story and we're sticking to it!

Dr Tony Lowther

Here I was in the countryside, kind of on holiday, getting an excellent education, no disruption of my classes at school. Frankly, I suppose, I had a wee titchy guilt complex about enjoying myself here when a war was on.

John Campbell Bennet

A friendship 'accommodated': Jean McDougall and Tony Lowther met at Cally School in 1939 and married in 1949 (Dr and Mrs Lowther)

Cally School had its own branch of the Home Guard – manned by callow youths rather than elderly veterans of the First World War.

We had a PT master in charge as a sergeant, and there were seven of us with one Remington 303 and a clip of five bullets to defend the Western World. My function as the runner when the Germans landed was to get down on my bicycle from the Observer Corps and knock on a certain window in a certain house to rouse the local butcher, who would then go ahead and organise all the rest of the war as far as I was concerned.

Willie Gilmour, Glasgow

Cally School Home Guard, with Willie Gilmour (back row, extreme left) (Cally House School Former Pupils)

I was quite sad to leave. I went to join up and went to the Land Army. Again I think that would stem from here. I was never a country girl. I was a town girl till the age of twelve and then I became a country girl and have lived in the country ever since. I have no desire to live in the city, and it was Cally that did that for me. It gave me a great lot of friendships, which I really cherish. You make friends along the road of your life but I think the ones I made at Cally will be the ones I remember forever.

Betty Pearson, Perthshire

MAIN PHOTOGRAPH:
Scapa Flow, the
traditional haven of
the British Home
Fleet, during the
First World War
(Orkney Library)

INSET: Lonely searchlight
operator on the
Orkney barrage
(Imperial War Museum)

CHAPTER 3

Bloody Orkney

Most of Britain had a quiet year until the evacuation of Dunkirk in the summer of 1940. But one remote place was buzzing with excitement: the Orkney Islands and Scapa Flow. The Flow, a huge area of deep water almost entirely surrounded by islands, was traditionally the safe anchorage for Britain's Home Fleet.

You couldn't help but be cynical about the situation in Orkney. In the First World War, they needed Scapa Flow in which to keep the fleet safe. Then the whole thing was allowed to decline totally. But as soon as the crisis of 1938 came, there was a panic to try to make it secure again . . . It was an exciting time when you were young. You saw the great battleships, the aircraft-carriers, the county-class cruisers and the destroyers. The Flow was full of ships that are long since gone, that one will never see again.

Ian MacInnes, Royal Navy, Stromness

Orkney's population of 20,000 more than quadrupled as the islands
became a floating fortress. But it was not a popular posting for the
60,000 servicemen.

All bloody clouds, all bloody rain,
No bloody kerbs, no bloody drains
The Council's got no bloody brains,
Oh bloody Orkney!
Everything's so bloody dear,
A bloody bob for bloody beer,
And is it good? – no bloody fear!
Oh bloody Orkney!
The bloody flicks are bloody old,
The bloody seats are always sold,
You can't get in for bloody gold,
Oh bloody Orkney!
Best bloody place is bloody bed
With bloody ice on bloody head,
You might as well be bloody dead,
Oh bloody Orkney!

Serviceman's poem, *circa* **1940**

A lot of them hated the place. With the fleet here, they had forty barrage
balloons in the sky at one time and the servicepeople would say, 'Cut the
bleeding balloons and let the islands sink!'

Johnny Pottinger, Lyness

We came ashore on Scapa Flow and it was terrible. The only place you
could go for entertainment was the local tavern – a hut, more or less,
with big queues outside. We were given jam jars as there were no glasses
to put your beer in.

Harry Dillon, Merchant Navy, Glasgow

My ship worked out of Scapa Flow. We went on the Malta convoys, we went
on the Russian convoys, to the North Africa landings, but we always came
back to the Flow. You imagine ports having shops and girls and dances but
there was none of that for us. Scapa Flow was just as bad as being at sea.
There was no shore leave worth having. So the captains decided that if you
couldn't give men leave, you could make them work – so we hung over the
ship's side painting the ship a different colour every day of the week in the
pouring rain! I thought it was the worst place I'd ever been to.

Derrick Johnstone, Royal Navy, Inverness

Scapa Flow was ringed with a barrage of anti-aircraft guns and I can remember visiting one of those up on the hills of Hoy, way off the main road. I suppose there'd have been a dozen or so men there and most of them were Brummies. They were stuck up in this place and the rain was coming down. There was nothing but heather and wet and cold and misery. Imagine that, men from Birmingham! We thought we had all lost our marbles, but when we saw them, we thought we were eminently sane!

Ian MacInnes

The lonely gunners, radar and searchlight operators were vital to the defence of the fleet. German bombers had proved they could attack the Flow and in the second month of the war, so had a German U-Boat. *U-47*, commanded by Gunther Prien, crept past the rusting blockships sunk during the First World War to fill the channels between islands. The battleship *Royal Oak* was torpedoed and sank with the loss of 833 men.

A Bofors gun crew near Stromness: have they lost their marbles? (Imperial War Museum)

There were sunken ships in the passages between the islands and nobody ever thought that anything could get through. They thought, in fact, it was sabotage to start with because they were quite certain that no submarine could have got in.

Joyce Anderson, Stromness

We were quite surprised because they had the blockships right across and wire between the ships and the shore. But I do remember that night thinking that it was a full moon and a high tide and that would be the night to try it. It was a marvellous piece of navigation to get through.

Sandy Wylie, Burray Island

Well it was a shock because everyone thought the Flow was impregnable. So Churchill came up and said, 'Get cracking, plug these holes'. And so the permanent barriers were built on his push and they were called the Churchill Barriers.

Walter Leask, Stromness

The Churchill Barriers, built throughout the war, finally made Scapa safe from submarines. But the fall of Norway in April 1940 made Orcadians fear the front line had reached their doorstep.

Number One Churchill Barrier plugged the hole that allowed U-Boat U47 to sink the *Royal Oak*. It replaced the line of blockships behind it (Orkney Islands Council)

I remember big ships loaded with servicemen arriving and we discovered it was the men being evacuated from Norway. They built a huge tented camp outside Stromness and put these men in and they weren't allowed out until Churchill had officially announced that Norway had fallen.

Joyce Anderson

The fear was the Germans would then come. And if they got Orkney and Scapa Flow then they could come down through the rest of Britain. So we had 'blood-red warnings'. On a Sunday morning we used to see the Home Guard – the old men – parading up and down the street. What would have happened if the Germans had come, goodness only knows!

Betty Garson, Stromness

When German planes did come, they met such a barrage from the guns all round the Flow. I remember seeing a plane caught in the searchlights and he dodged and he dodged until they eventually hit him.

Joyce Anderson

The WRI put on concerts and I remember one that seemed to go on forever. When it finished they announced that there had been a raid on the town and a plane had machine-gunned up and down the street. It was safer to keep us inside so, every time the barrage got too loud, they put the band back on to drown the noise. They had actually machine-gunned the roof of the hall.

Betty Garson

Manning the defence of the Orkney Islands was a posting to be avoided.

You can't afford to have a misunderstanding with a colonel – especially when you're only a private – so I was told: 'Gerry, you've had it this time, it's either Gibraltar or Orkney for you.' When I cast my eyes for the first time on the Old Man of Hoy, I was feeling very miserable. It certainly was a punishment because it was the start of a ghastly winter.

Gerry Meyer, Royal Artillery, London

Just a big nissen hut with one little stove in the middle and maybe about twenty to thirty beds in it. When you went to bed in the winter, you took your underwear with you so that it would be nice and warm for putting on in the morning.

Dilys Kelly, WAAF, Glasgow

Friendly Orcadians made life in a nissen hut more bearable. Many of these buildings are still serving Orkney farmers well (Gerry Meyer)

We had 280 men on a ship that was built for 180 so there wasn't much breathing space. So it was pretty miserable on the whole. It was probably better for the Army ashore or the Air Force because they saw people. I never met an Orcadian the whole time I was there.

Derrick Johnstone

The authorities made huge efforts to improve conditions, but for many servicemen it was the Orcadians who made life bearable.

Everybody was so sorry for them because there was nothing to do. We had the 'fourpenny bash' every day in the church hall where the men could go in and have tea and as much as they could eat for fourpence. It was the only place they had to go to be warm. Then everybody opened their doors. Everyone had 'their' servicemen and if one was posted he would come and say, 'I go away tomorrow. Here's someone to take my place.' When I was a child, it was a good excuse not to do your lessons because there was folk in every night!

Betty Garson

Even for the sailors stranded in the Flow, some rudimentary facilities were laid on in the main port, Lyness, on the island of Hoy.

When we got shore leave every fortnight, we went ashore at Lyness at four in the afternoon and came back at half past six. You could turn left at the head of the destroyer pier, go to the cinema and see a film and get a bacon and egg tea for one and six. Or you could turn right and go to the fleet canteen where you bought six tickets and that gave you six pints of beer for ninepence each. And if you were really flush you could buy one off another chap for a bob!

Derrick Johnstone

The theatre at Lyness had many of the stars of the day coming up to it – Flanagan and Allen, George Formby, Gracie Fields, Evelyn Leigh, Vera Lynn – and it was a great thing for the men who had no other entertainment at all. Someone told me that the Lyness cinema had the première of *Citizen Kane* before the West End of London. That was an indication of how keen the Admiralty was to keep the men happy.

Ian MacInnes

(Gerry Meyer)

When you went up there on an eighteen-month posting, you thought: 'Gosh, I will never last eighteen months!' But when it came to an end, we said: 'I hope I don't get a posting because I want to stay!'

Dilys Kelly

Women serving in remote postings enjoyed the status of wartime luxuries – scarcity value.

There were about five hundred Wrens – not enough because there were so many male servicemen. If you were taking a walk round the shore, you were tripping over courting couples.

Johnny Pottinger

When they did arrive, they were kept like precious ornaments. I think that it's highly unlikely that a sailor ever achieved the status of being capable of taking a Wren out. But if it did happen, I understand that he had to sign for her, and it was dated with the day and the time! So you see, it would have been very difficult to . . . [*laughs*]

Ian MacInnes

We had a very good social life up there because there were so many men compared to the number of Wrens. We had invitations to all the ship dances and all the concerts. We met a lot of different nationalities. They kept changing with the ships coming in and going out again. Some were nicer than others and our own boys at that time were shyer. They weren't so forward as the likes of the Norwegians or the Canadians. We had to be on our guard with any of them! I don't know how they behaved at

home or whether the girls were more protected, but we had to watch when we were out with a Norwegian – or a Canadian!

**Betty Gibson, WRNS,
Glasgow**

A unit of Wrens at Lyness on Hoy, with Betty Gibson (middle row, extreme right) (Betty Gibson)

Stromness was a very quiet place before the war. When the troops came it changed our lives altogether. We had dances nearly every night and there were about ten soldiers to every girl. It was very nice when you went to a dance because you were never a wallflower in those days.

Nora Meyer, Stromness

I was in the army of occupation and I got captured! I got captured by a Stromness lass. I met her at a dance, and there was a courtship and two years later we were married. The strange thing is that my wife's father was an Englishman and he came to Orkney as a Marine in the First World War and he married a Stromness girl.

Gerry Meyer, Stromness

Some of the soldiers unquestionably liked it very much and have continued coming up here on holidays with their families. Some even settled here. Others, of course, still hated it vastly. I can remember coming home on leave through Thurso. Another sailor said: 'Aye aye Jack, where are you going?' I said, 'I'm going to Orkney.' 'Oh, God,' he says, 'Orkney! What are you going to do there, are you joining a ship?' I said 'No, I'm going on leave.' 'God,' he says, 'here's a bloke going up there on leave!'

Ian MacInnes

Gerry Meyer, holding a poster, stands next to his wife-to-be, Nora. Gerry edited the services' newspaper, *The Orkney Blast*. He settled there after the war and became editor of *The Orcadian* (Gerry Meyer)

CHAPTER 4

Left in France

In 1939 the Jocks enlisted in their thousands.

It was always something to look up to – the kilts and the pipes. I loved all that. I'd march for miles for the pipes – gee whizz – I'd listen to the pipes all day! In 1939, they were going to put me in the King's Royal Rifles. 'Oh,' I says, 'You're not on. It's Scottish or nothing!'

Bill Crossan, Cameron Highlanders, Glasgow

The Scottish soldier, the Jock, whether he be Highlander or Lowlander, is held in very high regard. Don't let us forget that it was the Germans who gave them the label 'The Ladies from Hell' as a result of the kilt.

Derek Lang, Cameron Highlanders, Midlothian

Many of the Jocks recruited into the Territorial Army in the '30s were crofters and fishermen from the Highlands and Western Isles. Derek Lang was sent to double the number of recruits in the Cameron Highlanders' heartland in North Uist, South Uist and Skye in 1939.

I think there was tremendous enthusiasm all over the Highlands despite the First World War and all the scars that were left from that. Memories are short, mercifully, and people rallied to the colours in the most wonderful way.

Derek Lang

I joined because all my friends were joining. It was the best way to get a fortnight's holiday away from the island and enjoy yourself. And getting paid as well! I don't think it was patriotism. For some it might have been, but not as far as I was concerned.

Murdo MacCuish, Cameron Highlanders, North Uist

I joined when I was quite young. I was just sixteen and there wasn't much work to be had, just the lobsters in the summer.

Archie MacDonald, Cameron Highlanders, Benbecula

Gordon Highlanders march to Aberdeen station en route to France
(Aberdeen Journals)

Uist Territorials on annual summer camp at Barry Buddon, Angus, 1934. Archie MacDonald is second on the left
(Archie MacDonald)

It was great to have a summer's camp, but you never realised what was beyond that. You never realised that war was imminent.

Donald Alan MacLean, Cameron Highlanders, North Uist

In the hours leading up to the announcement of war, the Territorials were mobilised. Part-time soldiers became full-time. Instead of marching to summer camps in Angus, they were going to war.

I went in to see my brother, who was twenty-one years my senior. He'd been through the First World War, got caught up in Passchendaele, had a whiff of gas, was slightly wounded and was sent back into the line again. He lost a leg in the second Battle of the Somme in 1918. We just shook hands and, it may surprise you, but he said nothing. But, my goodness, he must have been thinking about what I was heading for . . .

Donald Alan MacLean

Donald Alan MacLean (top left) with other 'Uist boys' (Kenny MacKenzie)

I remember walking down the road with my mother right down to the pier. My mother never shed a tear. It was all laughter and joking. We all went away quite happy. We were quite convinced we were going to win this war.

Walter Kerr, Royal Artillery, Millport

We were only young lads. We thought, ach, Germans. We'll beat them nae bother. We never thought for a minute they'd ever bloomin' beat us! Never for a minute.

Bill Crossan

The 51st Highland Division was shipped to France in January 1940 to join the British Expeditionary Force. In March the Territorials were joined by the regular Black Watch, Seaforth and Gordon Highlanders, and in April were moved, under French command, to the Franco-German border. The Germans invaded France on 13 May.

They put us up in front of the Maginot Line. It was a phoney war. Then they sent us up to the front at Abbeville. And that was us – the 51st – strung right along the Somme to take the pressure off Dunkirk. Well, that's what I took it to be.

Bill Crossan

The ordinary soldier, the ordinary Jock, doesn't know what's happening. He's told to be here, be there, do this, do that. They don't know the ins and outs of where this or that company is. As far as I was concerned, we were in a cornfield in France.

Donald MacLean, Black Watch, Perth

Gordon Highlanders after a morning digging trenches on the Belgian border, spring 1940 (Imperial War Museum)

We didn't realise how poorly equipped we were until we came up against the Germans. The equipment we had was what they stopped using in 1918. Just one machine-gun per section, no tommy guns. The anti-tank guns we had were just like pea-shooters. They told us we were the best equipped army that had ever left Britain. We were soon disillusioned about that.

Murdo MacCuish

On 26 May, 338,000 men cut off by the German advance were evacuated from Dunkirk. The 51st Highland Division was left behind to fight a desperate rearguard action.

We actually attacked on the Somme. It was a disastrous attack. We hadn't got the equipment and the Germans had strengthened their forces by that time. We attacked under De Gaulle's command and we had French tanks and the Highland Division, but it was a disaster and we had to pull back from there, back to Saint-Valery-en-Caux.

Derek Lang

We went out from behind the hedges and the Gerries were shooting down on us. And the two French tanks – well, one got blown up and the other one ran away and left us out in the open. That was us snookered.

Bill Crossan

Hände Hoch!
A British prisoner captured on German film
(Imperial War Museum)

We were making our way back to Le Havre for evacuation, but we were cut off by Rommel, who came right round from the south between Saint-Valery-en-Caux and Le Havre and cut us off. We were surrounded there.

Derek Lang

I was in a sunken road. They said, 'The Gordons are coming up to relieve you in the morning.' It was just getting to daybreak, just semi-darkness. So I says, 'That'll be the Gordons.' I went through this hedge and this Gerry says, 'Hände Hoch!' Oh Jesus! I thought it was the Gordons. I couldn't believe it. And this boy at my back, he's saying, 'Let me through.' And I'm feart to move in case this German officer shoots me. All his men, they're all standing with hand grenades and everything ready to blow hell out of me. 'Oh,' I says, 'Hello, you're not on.' So I Hände Hoched!

Bill Crossan

We were pushed gradually towards Saint-Valery-en-Caux. And that was the famous morning of 12 June 1940. Precisely at 10.30 a.m. You could well ask if it had sunk in then. Well, it had then really. The business of surrendering your arms. That was the realisation.

Donald Alan MacLean

It was degrading for one thing. We were soldiers. We had been surrounded before and fought our way out. Here were thousands in the town – and thousands of French too – and I thought it was the most humiliating thing. I thought we should have fought on. I didn't realise how outgunned we were. I didn't cry, but I nearly did, I'm telling you. I was twenty and it was heartbreaking . . . marching to captivity.

Murdo MacCuish

I was completely shattered. We'd been trained on gunnery and gas and what have you, but never on what you do as a prisoner.

Jack Hunter, Royal Artillery, Millport

The town was on fire, in chaos. We made our way about five miles along the beach under the cliffs to see if we could get away in boats. But it was too late. The Germans converged from both sides. I was on board a little boat that was stranded on the sand and we were blown out of the water by the tanks. That was the end of it. It was quite desperate. The thought of being PoWs was beyond belief.

Derek Lang

Some prisoners escaped from the line as they marched towards Belgium and the Rhine barges which were to take them to prison camps.

An awful lot of Jocks did get away in ones and twos. When we got to Marseilles, there were hundreds of us who had got through in various ways. It may sound as if we did this on our own but if we hadn't had the most incredible support from very brave people – French farmers, peasants and townspeople – we couldn't have done any of this.

Derek Lang

Archie MacDonald, a Benbecula fisherman, escaped with his friend Roddie.

We made a bid for the coast thinking we could get a small boat. We were quite used to boats you see. And when we got there the

Derek Lang (extreme right) and other Scottish and French prisoners in this German photograph are seen being marched off the beach near Saint Valery (Sir Derek Lang)

Derek Lang, on the run, dressed as a French civilian (Sir Derek Lang)

Germans were there before us and had taken positions on the coast. It was all barbed wire. We tried to get through but when we touched the wire, tins started to rattle and they started firing at random, so we had to crawl away.

Archie MacDonald

Dressed as labourers, Archie and Roddie headed for Spain but encountered trouble from local youths in the South of France.

We left this café and there was a crowd of them waiting for us. We were talking the Gaelic and they couldn't make head nor tail of it. Roddie was tall and blonde and I was small and dark with the sun. They thought we were a German and an Italian and they got stuck into us and gave us a terrible hammering. Two men before us were caught by the Germans and they were talking in Gaelic. They gave them a map and the boys pointed to the middle of Russia. They got home too. So there's some use in the Gaelic after all!

Archie MacDonald

Donald Caskie, the Tartan Pimpernel, was running the seaman's mission in Marseilles and he had this arrangement with the Church of Scotland in Edinburgh in which he sent our names and addresses, and that was sufficient to say we were all right. The Church got in touch with our parents and that was my mother and father's first information that I was alive and kicking. I even have a letter from my mother sent to me in Marseilles. I still have it to this day.

Derek Lang

In Scotland, what had happened to the 51st Highland Division began to sink in. Around 8,000 Jocks were now prisoners of the Germans and more than 300 had been killed in action.

There was great trepidation then, because folk started counting on their fingers and wondering who had gone. There was always a loss of maybe one or two in every area, but we were never able to find out until afterwards who had been killed. The names were nearly all the same and I was afraid to go to the wrong house with a message about bereavement. I used to go to see people working locally just to make sure I didn't go with a message to the wrong person.

John MacInnes, local government officer, South Uist

It was a devastation. The 51st, the real 51st, gone. I was in the second 51st and I am sure that nobody that was in it would grudge the title of the real 51st to the Division of 1939 and 1940. And their loss hit everyone really hard. But I honestly never encountered defeatism, especially in the Scottish North-east. It was by no means a tradition of the North-east to acknowledge defeatism.

Hamish Henderson, Blairgowrie

General – later Field-Marshal – Erwin Rommel had commanded the 7th Panzers as they smashed into the Highland Division. He wrote in his diary:

I had the whole Division's fire directed on the northern part of the town, where, as we saw the next day, the effect was particularly devastating. The tenacious British, however, still did not yield . . . No less than twelve generals were brought in as prisoners, among them four divisional commanders. A particular joy for us was the inclusion among them of General Fortune, Commander of the 51st British Division.

The Rommel Papers

General Rommel and Highland Division Commanding Officer, Major General Victor Fortune, after the surrender in Saint Valery. This photograph was taken with Rommel's own camera (Sir Derek Lang)

The survivors were to spend almost five years in prison camps.

There is the feeling, of course, that there was an element of sacrifice, but it was all part of the operations plan, I've no doubt at all. But if you look at it from the prisoner-of-war confinement, it was certainly a sacrifice – in that you, as a young man, were to spend close on five years behind barbed wire, making the best of it – or the worst of it.

Donald Alan MacLean

They always seemed to pick on the Jocks. It's happened right through, hasn't it? Right through the Middle East and North Africa and Italy. They were always there, weren't they? They're a heavy lot. Don't know whether it was that wee dram that does it.

Bill Crossan

A Polish officer in
Scotland
(Imperial War Museum)

A Polish soldier waits for the
German invasion of Fife
(Imperial War Museum)

CHAPTER 5

General Sikorski's Scotsmen

German troops, guns and planes have crossed the Polish border to kill and destroy. The Polish army is already engaging the invader and Poland is ready . . .

War, **Pathe News, September 1939**

But Poland was not ready. Defeated in their own country, in France and in Norway, 25,000 Poles dug in for another stand – in Scotland. Scots were puzzled by the Poles' obsession with barbed wire, concrete and minefields. But these men – more than any other fighting troops in Europe – knew the power of the German war machine.

The Polish forces were to defend the part of Scotland from Montrose to Burntisland. This was the gateway to the very heart of Scotland. We were expecting the invasion to happen any time, so this coast had to be guarded day and night.

Walter Maronski, St Andrews

I knew very well from Prime Minister Churchill's speeches that he was going to make a stand in this country to the last soldier. But of course in the beginning when we arrived here there was nothing. We had to use the French arms that we brought with us from Norway. Everything the British had they lost at Dunkirk, so we were not very optimistic when we started. We knew very well what terrific arms Germany had. We were stationed for two years from Carnoustie down to Cupar in Fife. Our engineers built blockhouses and we were waiting for the German invasion.

Tadeusz Apfel-Czaszka, Edinburgh

St Andrews is a town which is known to be very sensitive about the most sacred place there, the Golf Links. And when we went there, what did we do? We absolutely devastated it. We built these big mounds with sandbags and we put the mines there and we had hand-grenade practice. Sometimes we thought *we* were the enemy and not the Germans!

Walter Maronski

Scotland reminded me of my part of Poland, especially the hills and lochs. I really loved Scotland.

Wladyslaw Wolanski, Edinburgh

Our impression of Glasgow was excellent. People opened their doors for us and even one day on a bus some stranger handed me a letter with a five-pound note inside. I could speak German and some people knew a wee bit. The hospitality was great to the Polish troops.

Tadeusz Apfel-Czaszka

Scottish people were very-narrow minded and they always thought that foreigners were intent on murder and rape. It had to be given out from the pulpit: 'Please remember that these men are our allies and invite them into your homes, make them welcome. They are tired of sitting in the barracks – give them a place at your table. They are some mother's sons.' I know of one lady in Dundee who was much touched by this story and she decided that she would write to the officer in charge of the Polish regiment that was stationed beside her. She wrote: 'I request the pleasure of your company for Sunday at three o'clock.' And he arrived *with* his company – *thirty of them!*

Bella Keyzer, Dundee

When you arrive in a country, you need to learn the language. I picked it up from the girls, mostly.

Tadeusz Apfel-Czaszka

The ladies were the best teachers of English and those boys who were the quickest in trying to sing to the birds were the first to master the English language. English was very difficult to learn and the ladies were really the best attraction for learning English and they were so helpful.

Walter Maronski

Curious Scots watch Poles march to the sound of a pipeband through Forfar (Imperial War Museum)

We were quite popular. Maybe due to our different manner to the British and, of course, a lot of the men in this country were abroad with the forces.

Tadeusz Apfel-Czaszka

They were the first men that I ever knew that used toilet-water, they were so clean and smelled so fresh. Our men looked upon them askance, because they used toilet-water. It was lovely, it was romantic.

Bella Keyzer

Well, let's face it. Our Scotsmen are not all that courtly, nice as they are. With the Poles, there was an excessive clicking of heels, kissing of hands and just general adoration of womenfolk – which we're not accustomed to here!

Isabel Morris, Aberfeldy

Polish troops at their camp in Crawford, Lanarkshire, 'sing to the birds'. Leo Dopierala is standing on the wall (Leo Dopierala)

I remember a fellow complaining to me about these foreigners coming here and stealing our girls. I couldn't accept that. They weren't his girls or my girls – they were *their own* girls. And he was the kind of fellow who couldn't have got a girl even if there hadn't been a Pole in Britain.

Cliff Hanley, Glasgow

There was a fight in Perth. It started with a few drinks and, of course, jealousy about the girls, and that was how it started.

Leo Dopierala, Perth

Yes, there was quite a good fight with the Black Watch, at the dance. After the fight we apologised to each other and exchanged flowers and that was it over.

Tadeusz Apfel-Czaszka

We went to a local dance somewhere, in this village hall and that was where I met my wife. We went about all the time together, but I never promised that we would marry any earlier, because I couldn't take the responsibility during the war. Then I kept my word. We got married in 1945 after the war was finished. I was married and so happy.

Leo Dopierala

General Sikorski, Commander of the Polish Army in exile, spent his time between London and his headquarters in Perthshire. Leo Dopierala was a member of his bodyguard.

General Sikorski was sometimes impatient and said he would have to be in Forfar at two o'clock and we had to keep to the speed limit. Forty miles an hour – that was the wartime limit. Of course, he was wanting to go faster.

Leo Dopierala

In camps throughout Scotland, Sikorski and the Commander of the First Polish Armoured Division, General Maczek, had regrouped their defeated forces.

His idea was to train the soldiers and prepare us – especially the tank regiment who were like a family. The five crew would be sleeping together, eating together and the morale was better. We all knew we had to win the war and go back to Poland.

Wladyslaw Wolanski

Leo Dopierala and his
Scottish bride,
Maidie Scott
(Leo Dopierala)

No matter how happy their four years in Scotland had been, the Poles still resented their exile. In 1944, as part of the allied invasion of Europe, they were heading home.

When I left this country and I saw the white cliffs of Dover, I thought I would never see them again. I thought the next stop would be free Poland, but that never happened. The war progressed very well and we had the famous victory at the Falaise Gap. Then in Holland the Germans made a stand and the Polish Division, for the first time in history, occupied part of Germany. But we knew by that time that we could not go back because the Yalta Conference sold Poland to the Russians and there was no way for us, especially those from eastern parts of Poland, to go back.

Tadeusz Apfel-Czaszka

At the Yalta Conference in 1945, Churchill, Roosevelt and Stalin had carved up post-war Europe between them. Many Poles wouldn't – or couldn't – return to a homeland under Stalinism, and resigned themselves to becoming Scots.

We were regarded in Poland as traitors and the Polish Underground Army was liquidated by the Communists. We had to arrange new lives here.

Walter Maronski

We just couldn't go back to Poland because we knew what would happen. We knew what the Russians were like. We felt betrayed and we didn't want to go back to Poland. A lot of our soldiers returned but many of them died in prison or disappeared to no one knows where.

Leo Dopierala

'Uncle Joe' Stalin's Russians were friends as well as allies to many on the Scottish left. They couldn't understand – especially in areas of Fife with a tradition of voting communist – why thousands of Polish servicemen wouldn't go home instead of competing for jobs in post-war Scotland.

The 1st Polish Armoured Division on the move
(Imperial War Museum)

At this time I was in Dunfermline and I wanted to get a job in the Dunlop factory which was very near where we were staying. And the man said: 'Sorry, no jobs for Poles in this factory.'

Jozef Mirczynski, Edinburgh

They were against us and they wanted us to go back to Poland. We heard this in every corner at that time: 'You have a free country, a good country and a socialist, communist country now, so why don't you go back?' Gradually, when people found out in this country what the Russians were like, things changed again, and the Polish generation and the Scottish community blended very well and we heard no more about it.

Tadeusz Apfel-Czaszka

If it pleased God to chastise us by exile, we accept it with humility and thank Him that He has chosen Scotland as the country of our exile.

Leo Dopierala

As long as we live
Poland has not perished.
We shall take back with a sword
What the foreign power has taken away from us.

Polish National Anthem

I still feel 100 per cent Polish and proud of my nationality. The old generation is getting pretty old now and, as far as the next generation is concerned, well they are more Scottish than Polish.

Tadeusz Apfel-Czaszka

Scotland's Polish warriors will eventually die out. But their names will live on in the exotic names of their Scottish descendants, and on their gravestones.

In Perth there is the cemetery of Polish war graves which was started in 1941 when the Polish forces came to Scotland. Seventy graves are reserved here for us, old men, like me, who want to be buried here. We will never go back to our country in this life.

Leo Dopierala

CHAPTER 6

Collar the Lot!

Thousands of Italians had settled in Scotland since the turn of the century. But when Mussolini declared war on Britain, native-born Scots began to ask, 'Whose side are they on?'

I feel myself to be Scottish first, but with strong Italian sympathies. I do not consider Italy as my country. I would never think of going back there. To me, Edinburgh is my home. I am as strongly anti-Glasgow as any other Edinburgh chap is. Whenever you hear Glasgow people calling us names, I can give it back to them hot! No, Edinburgh is my home.

Joseph Pia, Edinburgh

The Government wasn't so sure. At the outbreak of war, all 'enemy aliens' had been ordered to register with the authorities. They were labelled as Class A, B or C according to their estimated threat to national security. 'A's – Nazi sympathisers, about 1 per cent of enemy aliens – were rounded up at once. Among the 'C's were German Jewish refugees.

Scottish Italians collared for internment, June 1940. Joe Pia is towards the back left wearing glasses and a striped tie (Joseph Pia)

When you arrived in this country from Germany, you would actually visit the police and you were termed a friendly enemy alien, due to either religious or political persecution. Whatever you did, the police knew where you were.

Henry Wuga, Glasgow

As invasion fears grew, police, Special Branch and MI5 were given wider and wider powers to round up all categories of enemy aliens. In June 1940 Mussolini sided with Hitler and threw the fate of Britain's 19,000 Italians into the hands of the authorities. Two weeks later 4,000 were interned. Churchill had said in Cabinet: 'Collar the lot!'

It was a shame really. They should never have been interned. They were part of our heritage. They gave us fish and chips, they gave us ice-cream and they were a very hard-working community that kept themselves to themselves. One or two had little displays of maybe a clock with Mussolini's head on it in the chip shop, but that came down during the war.

Bella Keyzer, Dundee

Federico Pontiero with his ice-cream barrow in the 1930s
(Federico Pontiero)

I came here in 1920 and started off with an ice-cream barrow. I didn't take anything to do with politics at all. My father said to me, 'Never take anything to do with politics because it's one of the dirtiest games in the world.'

Federico Pontiero, Cambuslang

The Italian Government wanted Italians to keep their Italianinity and encouraged us to have sports activities and dances, so that the boys would meet the girls and they would inter-marry and keep up the Italian race.

Joseph Pia

I used to go over to Italy and all my friends over there said, 'Oh, you're not a good Italian if you're not a member of the Fascist Party.' In 1932 I was honoured with a membership of the Party. It meant you could go to dances, you could go to skiing, you could join anything in sport because it was just like the Labour Party here.

Renzo Serafini, Inverness

Renzo Serafini, kneeling in the centre, in Italy in the 1930s with friends in the Fascist Party (Renzo Serafini)

Most people accepted me fully, but now and again a person might call me 'Tally Wally', but not many. When the war started, shops were smashed up. The people who smashed up the shops didn't do it because they were anti-Tally or anything. They did it for looting purposes, purely and simply, for what they could get.

Joseph Pia

Some shops were set on fire, all the bottles of sweets were stolen and the police just couldn't cope because of the amount of Italian shops in Glasgow. Some who were not members of the Fascist organisation were coming to the police office and begging to be locked up because everybody knew they were Italians and they were frightened for their lives.

Alexander Bogue, policeman, Glasgow

I was interned and we had a young baby which was dying the night the police came. My wife was crying but the police said that I would have to go with them. I said to the inspector: 'I have been going out with a barrow all my days and I don't know anything about anything – Fascist or nothing.'

Federico Pontiero

Anyone who was Italian was taken in. Some were members of the Fascist organisation, but whether they were members or not they were all taken in. So Govan police office was pretty full up.

Alexander Bogue

The two policemen said: 'Blame Mussolini.' And I told them I knew nothing about Mussolini. They took me to the jail and the next day the baby died. The doctor came up and asked the inspector if he would let me out for five minutes just to go home to see the wife because she was in a bad state. But he wouldn't let me out.

Federico Pontiero

Even the most friendly of 'friendly enemy aliens' were picked up, including Jewish refugees who could have no conceivable loyalty to Hitler's Germany.

My parents were left behind in Germany. I sent letters to them via Belgium – this was before Belgium was in the war – and these letters were intercepted and I was accused of corresponding with the enemy, a technical offence. I was sent to the High Court in Edinburgh. I was found guilty of said offence and I was immediately interned. And the sergeant said to me, 'How old are you, laddie?' And I said, 'I'm sixteen and a half.' 'Oh,' he said, 'I cannae lock you up. Children under seventeen are not allowed in a cell in Scotland.' So, there was a conference: what are we going to do with this child? I was sent to a remand home for two nights, then I was sent to Maryhill Barracks, where I was with German merchant seamen who had been taken prisoner. In among those interned were my cousin, my prospective father-in-law, various people we already knew. And from there, eventually, we ended up in the Isle of Man.

Henry Wuga

Joseph Pia: 'There's nothing English about me!' (Joseph Pia)

In internment camps, Jewish refugees, Scots Italians, German and Italian merchant seamen and many others were gathered together. Officials found it all hugely confusing.

There were some members of the British Union of Fascists in some of the camps alongside we German Jews. And Vichy French officers who were allowed the run of the island, to which we objected strongly. Eventually the Fascists were put in a camp by themselves.

Henry Wuga

There was an officer there who said, 'Nationality? Naturally, English.' I said, 'English! There is nothing English about me. I am a Scot, or an Italian, or a Briton, but certainly not an Englishman.' Later on a fellow came across to me and shook hands, 'Well done.' I said, 'Who are you?' And he says, 'My name is Hamish Hamilton,' and I said, 'Oh, that sounds a very Scottish name. Why are you here?' And he said, 'I am a Scottish Nationalist.' I think that the British Government considered anybody who might interfere with the British war effort in any way whatsoever and got them out of the way. While I was there, there were three, four or five Scottish Nationalists, two or three Welsh Nationalists and a few Irish Nationalists.

Joseph Pia

The whole internment affair was quite frightening for people who had just left a country where there had been concentration camps. So, it was the same again. On the other hand, you're now imprisoned in a country which took you in – a country towards whom you feel friendly. I think it was an ill-conceived idea, but at a time like Dunkirk, sense doesn't always come first. There are decrees issued and decrees are acted upon. Churchill said in cabinet, 'Collar the lot.' And this is what the police did. And of course, anomalies arise.

Henry Wuga

Many women and young aliens had not been interned. But they were not free from worry about their fathers, brothers, friends and husbands.

That was one great worry – that there were a lot of Jews on an island and, if the Germans had come over, they were there for the picking. They had persecuted Jews and this is why we were here. We had thought we'd found freedom at last, and there we were. Well, I wasn't there, but my father, cousins – anyone you knew was there, and ready to be picked up and shipped to concentration camps. Once again.

Ingrid Wuga, Glasgow

The Isle of Man became virtually a prison island with capacity for 14,000 internees.

The Metropole Camp in Douglas, Isle of Man, housed over 600 mainly Italian internees from July 1940 until 1944 (Renzo Serafini)

They weren't camps in the sense of camps with huts. Seafront boarding-houses were encircled with barbed wire and became a camp for 500 or 1,000 men. We had no contact with the islanders, only with the soldiers and officers who were guarding us. That worked out pretty well because they could see we were not Nazis but people who came here for shelter, who would like to get out of the camp and join the army or help the war effort. To be locked up like that was a waste of productive labour.

Henry Wuga

Many internees wanted to fight fascism and campaigned to be released into the allied forces. But some – while not anti-British – felt that they could not agree to 'collaborate' in a war against their country of origin.

There were the collaborators and the non-collaborators. I just couldn't agree to that. I am as proud to be Italian as the Scots people are of being Scots. I couldn't sign that away.

Renzo Serafini

Interned sometimes indefinitely, the aliens were left to make some sort of life for themselves behind the wire.

In our own camp we had a German football team, an English team, a police team and a Scottish team. The Scottish team, by the way, was the best and a few of the policemen used to get a laugh because the one that they called the Scottish team all had Italian names. But we were the Scottish team for all that.

Joseph Pia

We had lots of writers in the camp, lots of musicians – the Amadeus Quartet was formed on the Isle of Man. These were people who had really reached the top of their profession, in science, in medicine, in music. These were all internees and obviously minds like this you cannot keep down.

Henry Wuga

There was a hotel where the Wrens used to stay and in the morning they used to go and do their exercises on the beach. They had these short skirts on and they were up and down like that, and all our boys had had a few years of not being near a woman and they were all very excited. They used to get a great thrill, everyone watching from the window.

Renzo Serafini

The way off the Isle of Man was via tribunals. If an internee could prove himself a 'friendly enemy alien', he could be released.

We found out that the English boys, every year, were allowed to go to Brixton and London to be questioned by a tribunal. But we, the Scottish boys, didn't. So I wrote a strong letter to the Secretary of State for Scotland asking why did the English boys get that privilege and what about us, the Scots?

Joseph Pia

The age of internment was eighteen and I was seventeen and three-quarters. On my last tribunal on the Isle of Man, I was told, 'We are not allowed to intern you, we cannot keep you a night longer'. I said, 'You should have thought of that before.' But then orders are orders.

Henry Wuga

...gistration Certificate No. 335439
...sued at Inverness.
On 8:9:39
Name (Surname first in Roman Capitals) SERAFINI Renzo
Alias
Left Thumb Print (if unable to sign name in English Characters).
Renzo Serafini

Nationality Italian
Born on 28:6:15 in Hawick Scotland.
Previous Nationality (if any)
Profession or Occupation Shop assistant.
Address of Residence 19 Young Street. Inverness
Arrived in United Kingdom on 28:6:15
Address of last Residence outside U.K.
Government Service
...port or other papers as to Nationality and Identity.
Italian Passport No. 046463 issued Glasgow on 16:9:32

Born Hawick, nationality Italian: Renzo Serafini's British papers (Renzo Serafini)

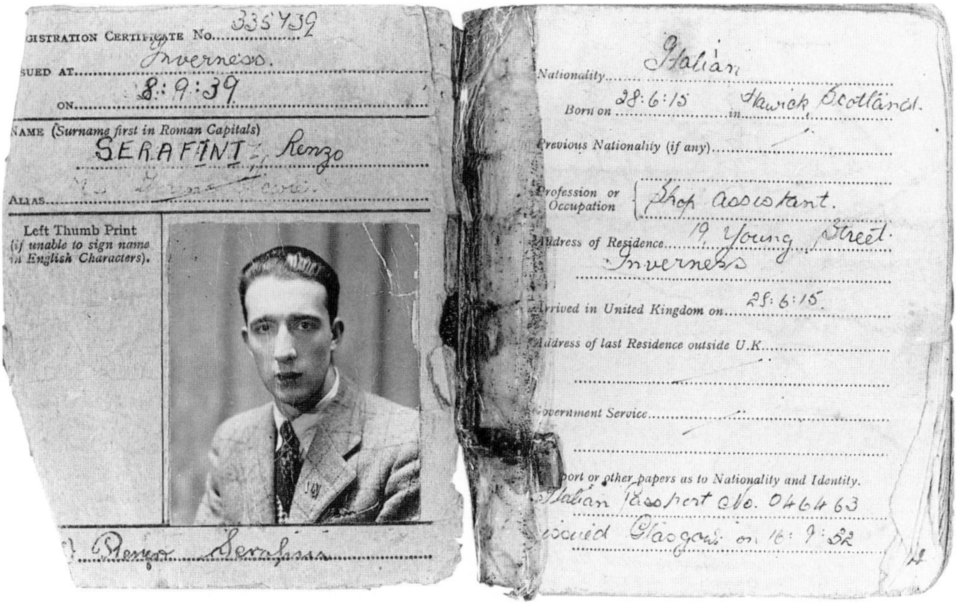

When I finally got home to Inverness, I met a Scottish officer I'd known as a boy. He said to me, 'I'm glad to see you're alive. What front were you in?' I said, 'I wasn't in a front, I was your prisoner.' He said, 'Didn't you sign for us?' And when I said no, he said, 'I'm proud of you, because no soldier should betray his country no matter how bad it is.' I had to wait for a Scotsman to pay me that compliment.

Renzo Serafini

Clydebank, the most heavily
damaged town in Britain
(*Herald/Times*)

CHAPTER 7

Blitzkrieg!

You heard about bombing in Coventry down south, but it didn't seem to affect us. I personally think we were living in a fool's paradise. Other people were getting it but we weren't. Then of course came the Clydebank Blitz. And it was like a bolt from the blue.

Hugh Savage, Glasgow

Glasgow, Greenock, Aberdeen and the coastal burghs of the North-east were all bombed during the war. But Clydebank had the sad distinction of being the most heavily damaged town in Britain. In two nights, on 13 and 14 March 1941, twelve hundred died on Clydeside, almost half of them Bankies.

Clydebank was an obvious Luftwaffe target. John Brown's shipyard and the Singer sewing-machine factory had been turned over to war production and the population instructed in civil defence.

I always thought a war was two sides in a big field wielding swords and things, but baffle walls went up for protection in the front of the closes and big steel girders went up inside the closes in case they would be blown down.

Kathleen McConnell, Clydebank

Luftwaffe reconnaissance photograph (Clydebank District Libraries)

Emergency sandbag protection, hastily built when war was declared, are now replaced by brick erections – a new feature of architecture so significant of the time in which we live that they are accepted by householders as a matter of course.

Tenement Warden, **Government information film, 1941**

They built these dreadful baffle walls outside all the closes and, of course, many a sore nose people got, me included. Think about it, no street-lighting and in the middle of the pavement a damned brick wall. Not unusual to have a sore nose!

Gavin Laird, Clydebank

Clydeside residents take
delivery of their air-raid
shelter in February 1939
(*Herald/Times*)

A year and a half into the war, Clydeside remained untouched.
Government observers interviewed members of the public:

'I see they advise you to take a gas-mask, but I think we're pretty safe
here . . .'

'It's England they're more for than Scotland . . .'

'I don't see how we can escape it. It's such a big industrial point . . .'

'I don't see that they can get through the defences if they're all that they
say they are . . .'

'I think that if we lie flat on the floor in our own homes, we're as safe as
anywhere . . .'

'We've all our plans made. The lady upstairs has the stirrup pump . . .'

'Well, I hope to goodness it'll come and be done with it and let
everybody's son and man hame. If it's got to come, let it come . . .'

'If they'd wanted to bomb Glasgow, they'd have been here before now . . .'

'I don't know the exact time, but when the better weather comes they'll
tumble for it . . .'

Mass Observation, *Report on Morale in Glasgow*, 7 March 1941

As Clydebank Cameron Highlander Tony Ventilla trained to fight
the Nazis, his Italian-born parents were arrested as enemy aliens.

They were taken to Barlinnie for interrogation. When I heard all this I went to my commanding officer and he wrote to the War Office to get them released, given the circumstance of me being a soldier. If I'd just left them alone, they would have missed the Blitz, but it wasn't meant to be that way.

Tony Ventilla, Clydebank

On 13 March 1941, more than 200 German bombers took off from airfields in Norway, Denmark, Germany, Holland and France. They converged over Loch Lomond *en route* to Clydeside.

On 13 March, I was late for school, but I didn't care very much because I was going to see a Shirley Temple picture that night with my friend.

Kathleen McConnell

I went to the pictures that night – a picture hall called the Palace – with two of my mates, the Doyle lads.

Gavin Laird

I was working overtime in John Brown's yard. I came out of the yard about a quarter to nine. It was a lovely moonlit night and I remember thinking to myself: 'What a lovely night for an air-raid.'

George Keane, Clydebank

Kathleen McConnell, aged seven
(Kathleen McConnell)

Well, the sirens went about nine o'clock and nobody really thought much about it because it had gone before and nothing had ever happened.

Kathleen McConnell

I heard the ominous sound of planes with laboured engines as if they had come a very long distance. And I said to myself: 'This is it.'

George Keane

We didn't go to the air-raid shelter that we should have gone to. I often wonder, would that have made a difference? But I don't think so . . .

Kathleen McConnell

The incendiaries started coming down and it was like looking at falling flames or rain that was on fire. If you are eight years old when you're seeing this happening, it's like some kind of horror film.

Gavin Laird

The bombing was fierce and the noise dreadful and it continued well into the night. The last thing I remember is my mother putting me to bed at about midnight, because I had school the next day. She tucked me in, you know, in the close and she went out for a breath of fresh air. That was the last time I saw her.

Kathleen McConnell

We had a wee sing-song to keep the spirits up. And as I was saying 'Who's next for a song?', we heard a terrible rushing noise and a dull thud. Not a bang but a dull thud. The next minute we were looking up at a huge red sky with broken girders and masonry above us and everything on fire round about us.

George Keane

I woke up and thought I was in bed. I went to turn but I found that I couldn't. I tried to loosen the clothes but found stones in my hand and they were hot. I shouted for my mother but there was no answer and the place was very still by now. My sister Lily heard me and told me what had happened and I could feel her underneath me. She told me to shout out very loudly because we would need to be taken out as the building was on fire. I heard someone say to Father White: 'We're going to damage her legs if we pull her like this.' Father White answered, 'We'll have to. She either comes out without legs or burns to death.' That shook me. No unconsciousness now. I worked very hard to loosen myself. They told me later that three ropes had been tied round me and each one of them had burned. My brother Joe came up with a stirrup pump and doused me with water because my clothes were singeing. And yet I haven't a burn mark at all. So I was very fortunate.

Kathleen McConnell

I got compassionate leave to try to find the bodies on condition that I joined a rescue service. I joined the fire brigade and where did they post me to? Napier Street, the street I'd lived in. It helped because whenever I came across a body I could have a look and know whether it was one of ours or not.

Tony Ventilla

I remember being carried through the streets in a stretcher and people looking to see who you were because they were all looking for their people. We were taken to Elgin Street School. That was horrific. My godmother, Annie Kirk, had a wee sweet shop at the corner of our street, and I saw her there with her arm severed from the elbow. She was screaming with pain, and she died. That was the first time I had seen anyone die.

Kathleen McConnell

I found a man whom I thought was my father and identified him. But it wasn't my father at all. He was taken out a week later. Later on, I found my brothers were still alive. One of my brothers, who was eleven years old, was sitting on my mother's knee when the bomb hit the building. We found him out in the street and yet they never found her body. There was her and, I think, three or four others who were never found. My wife was with my mother. We got her body out. She wasn't marked very much at all. She was fine. We were just married six months when I was called up. She was a Clydebank girl, the same age as myself, twenty-four.

Tony Ventilla

TOP: Rescuers digging in the ruins of Clydebank (Clydebank District Libraries)

MIDDLE: Unidentified Blitz victims are buried at Dalnottar Cemetery, Clydebank (*Herald/Times*)

BOTTOM: Dumbarton Road, Clydebank (Clydebank District Libraries)

I wondered why my mother hadn't been and I kept asking, but you didn't get a very good answer at that time because I suppose I wasn't ready. Father White came up and said that Joe and Lily were all right and that my mother and Hugh and Mary – those were the two eldest – had been killed and had already been buried in Dalnottar Cemetery.

Kathleen McConnell

I met people who lived in the same street. They seemed to accept that all these people were dead and that they had to carry on living. There were many sad cases. I went every day to St James's church hall to identify bodies and see if I could identify any of our own. There was a man there identifying just little bundles of things as his family. The man's name was Rocks and I think eleven of them there were his. It just made me feel that you think you are bad but you're not as bad as that . . .

Tony Ventilla

In the blitz on Clydebank, 534 people had died. Out of 12,000 homes, only seven remained undamaged. Every year in March there is a memorial service in Dalnottar Cemetery in Clydebank.

I don't think you should remember the Blitz with bitterness, because bitterness will get you nowhere. But you should remember it.

Kathleen McConnell

They always have schoolchildren singing at the service and I think it makes them understand what actually happens when nations go to war. It's a terrible thing to lose people close to you.

Tony Ventilla

At the ceremony a lone piper plays a lament, 'The Flowers of the Forest', and I think that's very appropriate. It reminds me of all those who were killed in the Blitz . . . 'The flowers of the forest are all wede awa'. . .'

Kathleen McConnell

CHAPTER 8

The Girl who Made the Thingummybob

It's a ticklish sort of a job,
Making a thing for a thingummybob.
Especially when you don't know what it's for!
But it's the girl that makes the thing, that drills the hole, that holds the
    spring,
That works the thingummybob that makes the engines roar!
And it's the girl that makes the thing, that holds the oil, that oils the ring,
That works the thingummybob that's going to win the war!

Popular song, c.1942

But in 1941 the war was not being won. At home manpower was a
million under strength. In December of that year, Britain became
the only combatant nation to conscript women – those aged
between twenty and thirty.

The giant Rolls-Royce Factory at Hillington in Glasgow built
Merlin engines for the Spitfires that defended Britain's skies and
the Lancasters that took the Blitz back to Hitler. It employed nearly
10,000 women.

I liked engineering. I loved the idea of these big enormous machines where
you could move handles and something valuable came out. The only
difference was that you'd applied your skill and intelligence and this valuable
thing went into an aero-engine which helped to win the Battle of Britain.

Agnes McLean, Glasgow

We used to get air aces to go round some of the factories and tell them
how their wee nut and bolt was holding the thing together when they
were having air battles. We got posters made for factories on which we
ringed the bit they were making so they saw how it fitted in to the
aeroplane.

Alastair Dunnett, press officer, Scottish Office

(Imperial War
Museum)

I was in the inspection department. The thing had to be just right because if it wasn't right at your end it wasn't going to be much use up in the plane! You had to be very careful.

Eva Collins, Glasgow

When I did my first component and got it right and passed the inspectress, I thought I was *an engineer!* I thought that was the greatest thing that had ever happened to me.

Mary Gray, Glasgow

I was directed into learning welding in the shipyards. This was heaven – what a difference from the monotonous clickety-clack of the weaving shed. Here was this ship being built, a thing of beauty. There was a pride in the job they didn't have in the jute trade. I dearly loved that job.

Bella Keyzer, Dundee

Inspection Department, Rolls-Royce factory, Hillington (Rolls-Royce)

It's a pretty grim place, a shipyard, and I would say the women workers brightened the place up a bit. There was no hostility at all in my experience. I think there were a few wee romances started as a result.

Hugh Savage, Glasgow

In a shipyard you work in all kinds of weather and all kinds of dirt and men are not just too particular where they do the toilet. There were no provisions for men going to the toilet, so they just did it where they stood and when you are welding on the top of this, oh boy! . . . and this is what I got paid twelve pounds twelve and six for! I worked ninety-two hours before I could get a man's forty-eight-hour rate.

Bella Keyzer

Hardly a man in sight: the Rolls-Royce factory floor (Rolls-Royce)

In 1940 a 'dilution agreement' allowed engineering employers to give jobs to women previously done by skilled men. After 32 weeks, the women were supposed to get the man's rate for the job. But throughout Britain employers found ways to evade paying up.

We were helping the war effort and we were all against fascism but employers were making a big bang out of us. They were making a bonanza out of exploitation of the women.

Agnes McLean

While women's skills forged ahead, their pay lagged behind – 50 per cent less than unskilled men. Agnes McLean first led the women in Rolls-Royce out on strike in 1941.

It was against the law to withdraw your labour. We didn't take that into consideration, we were about seventeen or eighteen. We were not considering anything except the fact that we were knocking our pan out and getting less wages than the guy next to us.

Agnes McLean

Opposition didn't just come from the men who ran the factory, but also at first from the men who ran the unions.

I was in the Transport and General Workers Union because the AEU, the engineers union, did not accept women. You had the five-year time-served men and they resented the women. Finally the unions began to break that down. The women were being used as cheap labour and the men realised we were undermining the whole wages structure.

Agnes McLean

In January 1943, 140,000 women were admitted to the AEU. By December, British trade unions were a million women stronger. But the equal-pay battle was not yet won.

There was the skilled man, the semi-skilled man, the unskilled man and there were 'the others', which were the women! Our first step was to start moving up the ladder, so we did battle for the male labourers' rate, even though we were doing fairly skilled work. What they were offering was a dead loss so then we went out on strike again in 1943. When we were marching through the streets people were shouting at us, forgetting the work we had put in.

Agnes McLean

Comrades in arms:
Mary Gray (front row,
extreme left) and Agnes
McLean (front row,
second left)
(Agnes McLean)

They were bawling at us, that their men were out fighting for the war and there we were going on strike, and I got a big tomato on the side of my face. I always remember that. They just didn't know the circumstances and maybe they just didn't want to know.

Mary Gray

They weren't standing at a machine twelve hours a day – or a night during nightshift – all those years, six days a week. That was when you weren't down in the air-raid shelters. We weren't standing for it. We were entitled to our money.

Agnes McLean

They got their money. A court of inquiry found Rolls-Royce had evaded the 1940 'dilution agreement'. From now on, pay depended on your job, not your gender.

The war had drained the Scottish countryside of young men. As German raiders mauled the Atlantic convoys, every cultivated acre became more and more vital. An army of women volunteered – or were conscripted – to feed the nation. *Land*

The Women's Land Army on parade in Union Street, Aberdeen, in February 1941 (Aberdeen Journals)

Girl was a Ministry of Information film starring real farmers and a real Land Girl and was part of the recruiting drive for the Women's Land Army.

Land Girls? I know about them. The men on the farm just hang around the dairy all day when they should be out in the field!

Land Girl, 1942

The real Land Girl in the film was Betty Reid, a farmer's daughter.

I was one of the first women in Scotland to join the Land Army. My number was number 12 and I used to be invited to recruiting parades in Edinburgh. I won the Royal Highland Society competition for the best plough-girl in Scotland. It's a most satisfying thing, ploughing a field!

Betty Reid, St Andrews

A lot of farm-workers resented Land Girls and weren't very nice to us. Especially city girls, who I expect they thought would know nothing and hold them back. But I think they found the city girls were just as good as the country girls.

Daisy Lundie, Glasgow

They built a hostel for twenty-four girls in Peebles and I drove them out to the farms in gangs and trained them. These girls were recruited from Edinburgh and Glasgow. They found it very difficult and unpleasant because they often got soaked to the skin two or three times a day while stooking or shawing turnips. But they were marvellous and got through a lot of work.

Betty Reid

Betty Reid in the film *Land Girl*. 'We'll make a ploughman of you yet!' (Imperial War Museum)

I was terrified. I didn't know what I was getting into. But when I had the choice of munitions in England, nursing or the Land Army, I thought, 'I'll go for the Land Army, it seems the easiest.' But it was very hard work. You had to carry animal feed on your back and you were up at five in the morning to get the cows in for milking. A girl from the town of Aberdeen was my interpreter because I couldn't understand a word the country Aberdonians were saying to me. They've got such a lot of funny words!

Daisy Lundie

I think the war was an opportunity for women to develop. Before that, your greatest aim in life was to get a husband. If he had a good job, so much the better, and if he was good-looking, that was a bonus! The war opened up a whole new vista and it gave women tremendous confidence. When they started moving into the Land Army, the forces or the factories, suddenly it was a whole new thing. It was great!

Agnes McLean

Ack-Ack ATS!
(Imperial War Museum)

(Imperial War Museum)

WOMENS ROYAL NAVAL SERV

join the Wren
free a m
to join th
flee

APPLY TO THE DIRECTOR W·R·N·S

CHAPTER 9

Manned by Women

Every man who can fight is needed for fighting, and it is up to the women of Britain to take over the non-combatant duties. *You* are needed in the ATS, in the WRNS, in the WAAF. *You* are vital to the offensive.

Call to Women, Pathé News, 1941

We really felt we could tackle anything. It was an opportunity to take over what until then had been a man's province. They were getting plum jobs, or the chance to use their intelligence and ability to the full, and here we were now getting that. It was a great opportunity for women and our efforts in the war certainly have paid off for future generations.

Muriel Gibson, Edinburgh

By 31 December 1939, 43,000 women had volunteered for the forces – not enough to release sufficient men for fighting. The Conscription Act prompted many women to volunteer so that they could at least choose their war work or their service. They could become 'Wrens' (Women's Royal Naval Service), 'Ats' (Auxiliary Territorial Service) or 'Waafs' (Women's Auxiliary Air Force). By 1943, over 443,000 women had donned uniform.

We got bombed out and we ended up in a room-and-kitchen, thirteen of us, four in a bed. I think that was the reason I volunteered – so that I could get a bed to myself!

Renee Weir, Glasgow

I fancied the Wrens' navy blue uniform and, being small and plump, thought the dark colour would make me thinner. If you had a father or a brother in the navy you got straight into the WRNS. Well, of course, I didn't. When I was interviewed, only the ATS was open and I didn't like the colour of the uniform. Then this woman said, 'I don't think you would be suitable in the army because they're all big strapping girls. I'll take you on as equipment assistant in the WAAF.'

Irene Milne, Edinburgh

There was a recruiting drive on for the ATS so I was in town and I said, well, it's now or never, so I just joined that. I know it was difficult to get into the WRNS. They were a bit snooty. Maybe I shouldn't say that?

Flora Armstrong, Glasgow

The army was the only thing I wanted. My mother didn't like it but then she wouldn't have liked anything that took me away from home.

Muriel Gibson

I went to the recruiting office and the man there said, 'Could you be ready to go on Thursday morning?' So I just said, 'Oh yes, yes, the quicker the better,' knowing that my mum wouldn't be able to keep me back or say anything about it.

Hilda Howden, Edinburgh

I left Waverley Station – with my mother and father and nearly all the people I worked with seeing me off. My mother and father were terribly upset so I had to keep up for their sakes, but honestly I was scared. What was I going into? I had never been away from home, never on a holiday without my parents. This was something awful.

Irene Milne

We had to take a jacket and skirt which approximated to one's size, and shoes which *they* felt were all right but which *my* tender feet didn't think much of. I remember that my skirt was too long and I had it almost under my armpits and tied with string round the waist and the jacket on top. I must have been a comic sight.

Muriel Gibson

I went for a medical and was told to strip. I thought, oh dear, and I poked my head out of this door and I said, 'Do I have to take everything off, even my pants?' 'Everything, I said!' replied the doctor.

Hilda Howden

There were about thirty to a hut, with one little fire at the end, and that was it. And the beds! I was picturing a mattress on a bed. It was three 'biscuits', three little straw squares. But I had it all to myself, right enough.

Renee Weir

Being on gun sites you were always away from civilisation. The sanitation was nil. The first toilet that we had was four posts in the ground, hessian drawn round it and buckets. And the big wagon used to come in every morning and empty the buckets.

Louise Wyatt, Glasgow

I was seventeen and three-quarters. It was quite difficult at first. I used to go into the bath at night and cry my eyes out. I think that lasted three or four nights and then everything fell into place.

Betty Gibson, Glasgow

We had an absolutely terrible WAAF officer in charge of us. Her eyes were always on you inspecting your uniform, the length of your hair, the length of your skirt, whether you were wearing the right bloomers underneath.

Irene Milne

Women operated almost half of Britain's barrage balloons.

Waafs training to handle barrage balloons. Early in the war there were doubts about whether women had the strength for the job
(Imperial War Museum)

It was hard work. We had to do wire splicing with all these thick cables and, I can assure you, we maybe went in with nice soft hands, but after that training our hands were really hard-skinned. There were twelve or fourteen girls to a balloon site. The bombers were coming over Glasgow trying to get the docks, so we really were busy. We didn't have an awful lot of sleep for quite a while. I was doing a man's job. Someone had to do it, and we proved that we could.

Hilda Howden

Even closer to the action were the women who operated the anti-aircraft batteries. Churchill, adamant that women should not kill, stopped them actually pulling the trigger.

We picked up the targets for the gunners and gave them the right bearing, so I suppose indirectly we did pull the trigger. We locked onto the target and that meant that the guns were moving with the radar dead on the target. So it was pretty good shooting then!

Louise Wyatt

Flora Armstrong: 'I ended up in the cookhouse' (Flora Armstrong)

You don't look back on the bad times, you only look back on the good times, don't you? Getting up at six o'clock in the morning, snow up to your ankles, under canvas, going to bed with ear-plugs in and pyjamas and socks, wellingtons lying at the side – you don't think about those times.

Renee Weir

I wouldn't have missed it for the world!

Louise Wyatt

Recruitment officers reported a 400 per cent increase in volunteers after they promised driving lessons as part of ATS training.

I said, 'I would like to learn to drive cars.' And she said, 'You'd better have a second choice.' I said, 'Well, I would like to go into stores or something.' I ended up in the cookhouse. There were too many people wanting stores and driving cars. I was one of the unlucky ones.'

Flora Armstrong

One thing women in the forces could be sure of was that they would get paid less than men.

Even as an officer one got very little at that time – and we didn't get the same as the men, of course. The argument was that we didn't have to take combatant duty. The men who were non-combatants might have to take a gun and fire it, whereas we would never be asked to do that. I had a captain working under me when I was a major's rank, and he was earning more than I was. I went on leave and he had to carry on the section in my absence. He said, 'I ought to get your pay, you know, while you're away.' And I said, 'Well, fine – you take my pay and I'll take yours!'

Muriel Gibson

I volunteered for overseas when I joined up. First we went to Delhi in India, then to Ceylon, then to Singapore. We still worked the same hours, sometimes very long hours, but there was time off to enjoy yourself. Going on leave was wonderful and you could see places you never dreamed of seeing before.

Elizabeth Aitkenhead, Ayr

Elizabeth Aitkenhead (centre) in a publicity photograph of the first Wrens to serve abroad (Lady Elizabeth Ross)

In India, Elizabeth met someone from her home town. Willie Ross was Lord Mountbatten's cipher officer and a future Secretary of State for Scotland.

We'd never set eyes on each other before, or even heard of each other. I suppose it was just because we were Scots that we found each other. There were very few Scots there. I know there were a lot of marriages during the war but I just had this feeling that it was better to go home and think it out carefully before you took the plunge.

Lady Elizabeth Ross

It didn't matter who you were or how good you were or how respectable you were, you still got the same name if you were in the forces – 'officers' groundsheets'. And it annoyed me very much.

Flora Armstrong

They thought that we had gone into the services just for the men's comforts. But I think they soon learned it was a different story.

Hilda Howden

If they became pregnant, they had to leave after three months. But it didn't happen very often – in fact, much less than in civilian life. Perhaps there was more opportunity in the army, especially in the mixed units. But

in the Ack-Ack, they were very keen on not having any criticism of their unit to be justified and they were very good.

Muriel Gibson

The WAAF has been a special thing in my life because I was very shy. If a man looked at me, I used to blush, I was so frightened. But the WAAF made me stand on my own two feet.

Irene Milne

No officers' groundsheets here! Flora Armstrong (top row, second left) and her unit of ATS (Flora Armstrong)

I think by the time VE Day came around we'd all had enough.

Hilda Howden

You missed all the noise, all the people around you, all the chatter. You went into your bedroom and you were alone.

Lady Elizabeth Ross

It was inevitable. You were bound to be discarded. There wasn't any need for you anymore. But it takes a wee bit of adjusting again to get back into civilian life.

Betty Gibson

I got married as soon as I came out and then I had my first baby. So I didn't really miss it that much, I was too busy. But looking back now, I'd rather have stayed in the army.

Renee Weir

Muriel Gibson – officer material – June 1944 (Muriel Gibson)

I went back to my old job in the education department in Glasgow. I wasn't settled because I wasn't doing anything responsible. It was made quite clear to me that as a woman I couldn't expect responsibility. It seemed absurd when I had been taking so much responsibility in the army in much more serious affairs to go back to this job and to be told that! So when the colonel I had last worked for wrote to me to ask if I would like to go back, I went back into the army and was very glad. I never regretted it.

Muriel Gibson, Retired Lieutenant-Colonel, Women's Royal Army Corps

CHAPTER 10

All Jock Tamson's Bairns

In the spring of 1940 the authorities thought that party politics – like stockings and bananas – was a luxury Britain could do without. An all-party National Government with Churchill at its head took over wartime Britain.

Brothers! There is one thing we must never forget at any time. Never to fall out with each other but work with each other as much as we can. Only this way can we obtain the ideal of smashing fascism! So let us keep all together, working for each other and never forget we're all Jock Tamson's bairns.

Shop steward addressing shipyard workers in *Clydebuilt*, a Ministry of Information film, 1943

You know there was this 'we're all Jock Tamson's bairns' thing. I found in the main that adversity really brought people together. The class divisions sort of disappeared for a wee while. But the politics didn't.

Agnes McLean, Glasgow

'Brothers!' Politics were not forgotten in wartime Scotland. This is a still from the film *Clydebuilt*, 1943 (Imperial War Museum)

'Jock Tamson's bairns' was the image of Clydeside that the Government wanted to believe in, but it feared that Britain's most militant area would concentrate on its favourite war – worker versus boss. It had enlisted the trained 'observers' of the social research group Mass Observation to monitor morale in industry. A week before the Clydeside Blitz, an observer wrote:

It would be facile to suggest that 'What Glasgow needs is a few bombs' . . . A number of highly placed persons in Glasgow used the above bomb argument and said that nothing else would do any good . . . It is *extremely unlikely* that the Germans will, after leaving Clydeside alone for months, kindly oblige by dropping just enough bombs to stiffen morale . . . It is not that Clydeside workers are against the war or for peace . . . It is rather that Clydeside workers are *also* having a war of their own, and that they cannot forget the numerous battles of the past thirty years.

Report on Morale in Glasgow, 7 March, 1941

There was always the feeling that if you made too many sacrifices you could never win them back again when the war finished. The workers shelved their demands because they wanted to make a contribution to the war effort. But I feel that the sacrifices were one-sided. The employers were on costs plus 20 per cent, so no matter what happened, they were getting 20 per cent of what the job cost. But the workers' basic wage never changed for the whole five or six years of the war.

Hugh Savage, shipyard worker, Glasgow

The wartime slogan 'Go to it!' attached in a pamphlet from the Clydeside Apprentice Committee, March 1941 (Hugh Savage)

The conditioning of years, plus the always militant background, has produced a scepticism among many of the workers which is more deep and more bitter than anything we have found anywhere else. There is a strong feeling that after the war the scrapheap will be higher than ever.

Report on Morale in Glasgow, 7 March 1941

Conditions really were primitive in John Brown's, as in every other yard. In the '30s, workers were queuing up to get a job and they didn't need to worry about conditions. I must tell you that the toilets were Victorian toilets – they had to be seen to be believed. You had a trough and about thirty people sitting on it and you had spikes behind the seat so that if the worker was stupid enough to lean back, the spikes would go into their back – that was the mentality of the employers in the yard. That was their attitude to the workers.

Hugh Savage

Quite a lot of men still hate their bosses, just about as much as they hate Fascists. Quite a lot of bosses are hating their men nearly as much as they are hating Hitler.

Report on Morale in Glasgow, 7 March 1941

The heavy air attacks on Clydebank have improved the atmosphere in so far as they have brought the reality of war nearer. But there is little evidence to suggest that they have fundamentally altered the situation.

Glasgow Report, 3 April 1941

I felt I was involved in the class war, because at that time I was in the Communist Party. They had a tremendous dispute going on because one side of the Communist Party thought that we shouldn't be participating in a capitalist war. The other side was, 'Well, we are fighting Fascism.'

Agnes McLean

You didn't allow the management to ride roughshod all over you because the workers weren't as daft as that. But when Russia came into the war, we probably didn't fight as hard as we had before. There was a definite change. We were sending ships out of Clydebank – they were going to fight for 'Uncle Joe Stalin'. Everybody called him 'Uncle Joe'. They wouldn't call him that now, but they called him it then.

Hugh Savage

All over Scotland, many politically active people were spied on.

I was followed everywhere. Sometimes when I went to Party meetings in Kirkcaldy you could look up and see a lad with a camera photographing everybody going in. Even when you went to the pictures with the wife, he'd always be there.

Jimmy Miller, miner, Leven

Like Communists, Scottish Nationalists were treated with suspicion.

My friend, Jimmy Bennett, formed the Local Defence Volunteers and drilled them in proper army style until the Home Guard was formed. Then Jim was told never to come back. He was a Scottish Nationalist. When the Home Guard got guns, Jimmy was out!

Jimmy Miller

There were those of us who, like myself, joined the army to fight against the tyranny of Hitler. There were others who felt Scotland was being dragged into the war at England's tail and they resented that. A lot of people who didn't want to join the army weren't conscientious objectors as such – but were objecting to Scotland not having a say in the matter.

Muriel Gibson, Edinburgh

Rona Black at the SNP's Wallace Rally at Elderslie, 22 August 1942. With her, from left to right, are Alex Sloan MP, R.E. Muirhead and Arthur Donaldson (Mr and Mrs Taylor)

I was not really interested in fighting for King and Country at all. I was prepared to fight against fascism, but not to fight for King and Country. The fellow behind the counter said, 'I'll just register you as a conscientious objector.' I said, 'You can enrol me with the Salvation Army if you like, but I'm not going to be conscripted. I'm going to join the Merchant Navy and that's that.'

Ronnie Taylor, Nairn

My father edited a nationalist newspaper, *The Free Man*, and he said he didn't want to fight for England – Scotland is different, we've got our own nation. He used to help a lot of young people who were on the run. He was under suspicion because of his journalism and the house was ransacked several times by MI5.

Rona Black, Nairn

While there is much admiration and sympathy for the people of London especially, most people here talk as if that was almost another war . . . This lack of close identification with the English war is clearly a dangerous tension . . . and is indeed in line with much unformulated and largely unconscious Scottish thinking about the direction of unity and loyalty.

Report on Morale in Glasgow, 7 March 1941

Arthur Donaldson, a prominent Nationalist who was opposed to Scotland's involvement in the war, was interned in Barlinnie Prison, Glasgow, because MI5 believed he was a Nazi agent.

Muriel Gibson had helped Donaldson with some secretarial work.

At six o'clock in the morning, I had just woken up when two strangers came in – a man and a woman – and it turned out they were from the police. They examined all my belongings and all my papers and books and then took me down to the police station. What they wanted to know was not what I'd been doing, because obviously I'd been doing nothing. But they wanted to know what Arthur Donaldson had been doing and they said he was a spy. I said he wasn't, not in any way, he was a Scottish patriot. I was at the police station all day and I was rather frightened. After the interview they let me go. But I heard long afterwards that I had been 'tailed'. This was slightly embarrassing for me as I had been going out with one of the warrant officers then. You know, sitting chatting on the canal bank until all hours. I don't know what fun it was for the onlooker!

Muriel Gibson

Since early in the war, women had been conscripted into industry. But in the summer of 1943 the Government began directing what it called 'surplus unskilled woman labour'. Scotland exported convoys of women – unmarried and in their twenties – to the factories of the English Midlands. Betty Collins complained to the Minister of Labour.

I resented it very much and wrote to Ernest Bevin saying that I didn't see why we should go down there when I was quite sure there would be work available in Scotland where we actually came from. He pooh-poohed the idea.

Betty Collins, Glasgow

We were fighting against Hitler, who was drafting labour from one place to another, out of their homes to a foreign country and here were we doing the same. I think it was really a sense of terrible outrage that they were doing that because they should really have used them in our factories at home. And it meant, too, that you lost people out of Scotland forever.

Muriel Gibson

When you think back now, you think how ignorant you were in accepting

Women sign on at Glasgow Labour Exchange for war work after the passing of Ernest Bevin's Conscription Act (*Herald/Times*)

being taken away like that – without a fight! May I say that we were just like cattle getting herded. It was a horrible experience.

Betty Collins

I remember one morning a girl was testing some mercury and it blew her to bits – that whole part of the factory was blown out. It was dangerous, really dangerous. You got one-and-six a day added onto your wages in the danger zone.

Ina Collins, Glasgow

The most dramatic demonstration of Scottish resentment happened in Glasgow in the winter of 1943. Six members of a nationalist youth organisation bombed and slightly damaged the headquarters of ICI in Blythswood Square.

Two of our members were in the Home Guard and had access to hand grenades. We just blew up the headquarters of ICI. That was the first target we had selected, but we were planning several other things like employment offices, where they were taking Scottish girls to work in horrible conditions in the middle of England. But unfortunately the movement was betrayed and our programme was stopped short with our first demonstration. Three people involved in collecting the hand grenades got nine months and the others got eight months. We were actually expelled from the SNP for bringing it into disrepute.

Ronnie Taylor

A nationalist alliance: the wedding of Ronnie Taylor and Rona Black (Mr and Mrs Taylor)

People were saying, 'That was a great thing to do for Scotland.' It made the southern MPs and all the rest realise that our girls didn't want to move down south. There was tremendous adulation for the six boys – I married one of them in the end!

Rona Taylor

We saw our girls (500 of them per week) being drafted away to work in the new factories in the south. Unless drastic and immediate steps had been taken to correct these drifts to the land beyond the Cheviots, the outlook for Scottish industry and the Scottish nation post-war had been bleak indeed.

Tom Johnston, *Memories*, 1952

Tom Johnston shared the concern of the young Nationalists – and, as Churchill's choice for wartime Secretary of State for Scotland, was in a position to do something about it. One of the original Red Clydeside

MPs, Johnston had served in two Labour governments in the 1930s, but, disillusioned with the compromises of politics at the highest level, was about to retire – until Churchill got his hands on him.

I suppose a rabbit cornered by a boa-constrictor would have had just about as much chance of escape. In the end I was bundled out a little bewildered but buoyed up by the knowledge that I would be given the chance to inaugurate some large-scale reforms under the umbrella of a Council of State which, if we emerged as a nation at the end of the war, might mean Scotia Resurgent!

Tom Johnston, *Memories*

In 1909 Tom Johnston wrote *Our Noble Families*, a savage attack on the Scottish aristocracy. In 1941 Churchill counted on Johnston's left-wing credentials to avoid the 'Red Clydeside' agitation of the First World War (Mary Knox)

He immediately saw that here was an instrument through which he could bring to some success his great hopes for Scotland. The Council of State consisted of all the former Secretaries of State for Scotland of all parties. Churchill agreed that if the Council came to a unanimous decision that something was good for Scotland then he would go along with it. Tom's idea was that if all the factions put their demands on the table maybe three would be unanimous and, if you push them through, maybe the next three will not be so difficult.

Alastair Dunnett, Tom Johnston's press secretary

Throughout the war, the Scottish National Party did well in by-elections. Johnston used the nationalist threat to prise concessions out of Westminster. Home Secretary Herbert Morrison wrote:

He would impress on us that there was a strong nationalist movement in Scotland and it could be a potential danger if it grew through a lack of attention to Scottish interests.

Herbert Morrison, *An Autobiography*, 1960

He leaned over the Cabinet table – I remember him telling me this gleefully the next day – and said, 'Prime Minister, if I don't get my way on this I'm gonny get the 51st Division, when they come home, to bring their bloody bayonets!' Well, he got his way!

Alastair Dunnett

Johnston's Council of State realised that Scotland's post-war prosperity depended on its wartime industrial base. In February 1942 Johnston set up the Scottish Council on Industry to attract war industry north.

Pre-war planning had rather dismissed Scotland's industrial capacity, apart from shipbuilding, and was trying to concentrate industrial production in the Midlands and the South of England. And this was one thing that Tom resented very much and fought fiercely against. Under the UK approach, Scotland would never have got a fair share of what was going.

Alastair Dunnett

Johnston's Council attracted 700 new enterprises and 90,000 new jobs. The intense effort of war production took its toll on the workforce. There was no National Health Service, but Johnston had his own scheme.

Hospitals had been built in the late '30s on the assumption – which proved wrong – that many hundreds of thousands of people would be killed or injured. They were empty and well staffed, so he poured the people into these places.

Alastair Dunnett

The success of the experiment – by April 1945 we had wiped out the waiting lists of 34,000 patients on the books of the voluntary hospitals – was such that our scheme had been extended from the Clyde Valley to all of Scotland and blazed a trail for the National Health Scheme of post-war years.

Tom Johnston, *Memories*

He thoroughly enjoyed being Secretary of State. He enjoyed getting things done which he probably never would have done if he had been in the Labour Government. Once I went to a Downing Street reception with my father – rather under protest from him – and Churchill greeted him, with the words 'Ah, here comes the King of Scotland!' I shall always remember that.

Mary Knox, Tom Johnston's daughter

Despite its total war economy, the British Parliament guaranteed £30 million to bring electrical power to the remote glens of Highland Scotland.

A few shameless Twelfth of August shooting tourists, who themselves took care to live in the electrified south for eleven months in the year, moaned about the possible disappearance in the Highlands of the picturesque cruisie.

Tom Johnston, *Memories*

In some of these lonely cottages they bridged the gap from the cruisie and the oil-lamp to electricity in just one bound and that was a great thing because then post-war industries could be serviced by lavish supplies of electricity.

Alastair Dunnett

The end of the war brought the end of Churchill's National Government. Johnston did not stand in the 1945 General Election, but he continued to serve on various public bodies such as the Hydro Electric Board.

The Hydro Electric scheme went through the House of Commons without a division. It was a ruthless, magnificent piece of aggression. Along with Tom's other wartime achievements, it gave people in Scotland an expectation of a better time. He was the greatest man I have ever worked alongside. He was the only world-class statesman that has entirely and utterly devoted himself to Scotland.

Alastair Dunnett

His main object in life – as far as I was concerned – was Scotland. His radicalism was needed when he started in politics and that was probably watered down a bit, but he was still a Socialist when he died. I have no doubt about that.

Mary Knox

I have become uneasy lest we should get political power without our having an adequate economy to administer. What purport would there be in our getting a Scots Parliament in Edinburgh if it has to administer an emigration system, a glorified Poor Law and a graveyard!

Tom Johnston, *Memories*

Opening of Loch Sloy Power Station, 18 February 1950, with Tom Johnston standing to the right of Queen Elizabeth
(Hydro Electric plc)

CHAPTER 11

Don't Sit Under the Apple Tree

Don't sit under the apple tree with anyone else but me,
Anyone else but me, anyone else but me.
Don't go walking down lovers' lane, with anyone else but me
Till I come marching home.

Andrews Sisters' song, 1942

War brought together young men and women who would never have met during peacetime. Old patterns of love and marriage broke down and the Andrews Sisters' advice went unheeded.

Early in 1940 foreign servicemen began to regroup and train in Scotland. By the late spring of 1944, Britain played host to 1,421,000 Allied troops.

The most romantic thing I knew of was the Dutchman who courted girls with one of our love songs, *My Love is Like a Red Red Rose*. It was beautiful to think about Rabbie's words getting used by a Dutchman – when our men said, 'Hello hen, how are you doing?' I myself married a Dutch sailor.

Bella Keyzer, Dundee

Then the Americans came. The Americans were top glam because they were straight from Hollywood, every one a film star. They had terribly smart uniforms. Even the privates wore ties and they were loaded with dough. The girls really went for the Americans. You could get a lot of goodwill for a bar of chocolate at that time.

Cliff Hanley, Glasgow

Six-foot, handsome as a film star, GI Jim Johnston *looked* the part.

I arrived in Glasgow, stepped off the train and a girl came up and said: 'Carry your bags, soldier?' And I said: 'Awa' and boil yer heid!' And she

OPPOSITE:
GI Jim Johnston, left
(Jim Johnston)

OPPOSITE (INSET):
Shortly before D-Day a
Jock walks out with a
Land Girl
(Imperial War Museum)

nearly fainted when she saw me in my American uniform answering her back the way I did.

Jim Johnston, Glasgow

Jim's family had emigrated to the USA – where Jim was born – in 1926. During the Depression, they came back to Scotland. In 1943 Jim received his call-up papers from the President. Apprentice Jimmy became GI Jim.

There was always an immediate double-take –'Where the hell do you come from?' It always seemed odd to me that there were all these guys called Chapanski, Jagowski and Lafamina – and I'm Johnston and I can't make myself understood! I remember my brother was in the British Army and he had seven shillings a week. I was getting seven *pounds* a week! And it was a big deal then – taxis everywhere, out for lunch, staying in hotels. We were bringing out the fivers and going to the Locarno and buying drinks. When I was an apprentice we couldn't afford to buy drinks for women. It was hard enough buying a drink for yourself.

Jim Johnston

You got a reputation if you were continually seen with Yanks. You saw girls ogling them, hoping they would ask them to dance because there was always chocolate or a pair of nylons at the end of it. But some of us thought it was just a wee bit cheap – and unfair, because some of these boys were a long way from home and I suppose they were wanting some sort of companionship.

Chris MacKay, Edinburgh

The influx of eligible, high-spending men had a disastrous effect on many relationships.

There must have been an awful lot of disappointments when husbands finally got home. I remember one woman up the next stair. Her husband chapped the door and her 'friend' had to do a bit of running about – under the bed! She nearly died! I don't know if her husband ever found out. I suppose he did. His mother lived in the same stair!

Margaret Docherty, Glasgow

There was a certain amount of carelessness in the way we behaved then. You were here today and you didn't know if you were going to be here tomorrow. A lot of people got married who maybe shouldn't

GI Jim with his Jock brother (Jim Johnston)

have. In my case, I went into the factory and I was taking up a lot of trade union activities. When my lad came back, he was a stranger, a total stranger.

Agnes McLean, Glasgow

Prisoners-of-war – like the men of the 51st Highland Division captured after the fall of France – spent five years wondering about their loved ones.

I sent my girlfriend a letter saying, 'I don't know how long I'll be here darling. You better break it off.' I knew it was going to be a long time. She got married, although I was always hoping she wouldn't. She said, 'What else could I do, Bill?' And I said, 'Quite right darling.' So that was it. That's life.

Bill Crossan, Glasgow

But Stuart Brown found romance in this unlikely setting – doing forced labour on a German farm in Poland.

We became very much part of the community and they treated us as normal human beings. They gave us a Christmas tree. After the celebrations were over, the farmer's daughter came and spoke to us prisoners. She was practising English. It developed from there.

Stuart Brown, Edinburgh

I liked him straight away. We used to meet in the farmhouse kitchen because the prisoners used to come and warm themselves there, but it was very dangerous because there was always a guard about. It wouldn't have been very good for a German girl to be caught. My father was very worried and he said: 'You're wasting your time, child. You will never be able to go to Britain.'

Dora Brown

As the Soviet Army advanced through Poland, Dora's family fled, taking Stuart with them. In the chaos of the battle for Danzig, Stuart and Dora became separated from her family.

The first Russian I met asked me how many Russians I had killed in the war, even though I said I was British. The second one stuck a revolver in my stomach, marched me off and pinched my boots. So I treated them with a degree of caution. The first night they were in Danzig there was rape and pillage. We saw the way the wind was blowing so Dora and I hid under a bed. We could have made a better choice because they brought in a woman and several of them raped her.

Stuart Brown

We knew that we might not be so lucky the next night. I put on prisoner-of-war trousers and I cut all my hair off and made my face dirty. The Russians liked a fresh young woman – that's who they were after.

Dora Brown

At the end of three months, we heard that the British were in Berlin and we'd also by that time met other prisoners-of-war, one of whom had married a Polish girl. We did eventually reach Berlin, dodging the Russians on a refugee train. They took us to a displaced persons' camp and the first British officer I saw gave me a row for bringing Dora with me. He said she had to take the uniform off – she had no other clothes – and go back from whence she came. So I just said 'Well, I go back as well.' But luckily he was transferred and the man who succeeded him was most understanding.

Stuart Brown

A working party of Highland Division PoWs, with Stuart Brown (front row, second left) (Mr and Mrs Brown)

At the beginning of December 1945 Stuart got an order to go home and I had to stay behind. He wrote to local MPs and the War Office to get permission for me to follow. At the beginning of February 1946, I got a wee paper which allowed me to come to this country. In the train from Dover to Berwick it sounded as if the people in the compartment kept using the word 'German'. I got really worried and felt I would like to go back. But I was so much in love – and, after all, I had nowhere to go back to. The Russians took my father away and later we heard he had died in a Russian labour camp. I was worried about how people might receive me. But the Scottish people were always really very kind, friendly and understanding.

Dora Brown

Dora in 1941
(Mr and Mrs Brown)

Jim Dickson had joined the Tank Corps in 1939.

First taste of action was in 1941. In 1942 we were 'hands up' in Tobruk. How did it feel? Blinkin' terrible.

Jim Dickson, Kirkcaldy

Jim was sent to a PoW camp in Italy. When Italy capitulated, Allied prisoners feared being shipped to Germany. Jim bribed his way past the Italian guards and spent three weeks dodging German troops. Outside the village of Grotta Azzolina, he asked a young farm girl for help.

The way he spoke and was dressed, I thought he was maybe out of a mental hospital. My sister said, 'Poor boy, he will be from the camp.' She was a very brave girl and asked him for lunch. He got to wear my brother's clothes and we washed what he was wearing. Jim spotted my brother's bedroom and said, 'Maybe I could sleep here.' So my mother said, 'You can stay tonight but tomorrow morning you must go. You can't stay.' Every time I passed him, I saw his blue eyes looking at me. My mother went to the chapel and came home full of strength and said, 'We are Christians and we must try our best to save this boy. I am a mother myself. Girls, we'll keep him. The British will arrive in two weeks time.'

Peppina Dickson

Peppina's family eventually hid Jim for ten months.

I opened the shutters and there were Germans surrounding the house. I thought, 'God, I've had it. This is my last night.' I knew they would have shot me. So the girls prepared the cesspit – where all the dung goes – to hide me in! We cleaned it out and put straw in it and a covering over it. I couldn't sleep and was soaking with sweat.

Jim Dickson

Well, he was more dead than alive in the morning because there was no oxygen in there. And the smell! And he said to me, 'No way could I face another night, not even another hour in there. I don't care if the Germans catch me.' I loved Jim as a brother. At the end of the ten months, he said he loved me, but not just as a friend. But he said he could never ask me to marry him because he had nothing in Scotland. I loved him more for his honesty when he confessed that. So then we went to see the priest.

Peppina Dickson

TOP: A postcard home to Jim Dickson's mother in Fife (Mr and Mrs Dickson)

BOTTOM: Jim Dickson, Peppina (left) and her mother and sister (Mr and Mrs Dickson)

He asked her religion and she said, 'Catholic.' And he asked me and I said, 'Church of Scotland.' 'Oh,' he said, 'you'll never get married, you'll need to get dispensation off the Pope'. I said, 'The Pope! You can't even contact the next village. I've no chance!' About a week later, I said, 'Come on, we'll go into the village again and this time I'll be a Catholic.' So we went to get married at nine o'clock at night. They rang the festa bells and the church was packed.

Jim Dickson

On 4 June 1944, Rome fell to the Allies. Throughout southern Italy, the Germans were in retreat. Ten months later, Jim and Peppina were on their way to a new life in Scotland.

Hong Kong, Christmas Day, 1941. Royal Scots officer Drummond Hunter lay in a hospital bed with a broken back. He had been wounded in the battle to defend Hong Kong from the Japanese. His fiancée Peggy, a volunteer nurse, was at his bedside.

This was when we decided that perhaps if we got married they might keep us together. The senior chaplain to the forces was there so we asked him if he would conduct the ceremony.

Drummond Hunter, Edinburgh

I thought perhaps I could go and put on my white uniform and then I could actually be married in white. I never even had time to do that. Drummond was lying flat on his back covered with a sheet and we all stood round his bed. The ceremony began and about three-quarters of the way through there was a tremendous crash of bombs and automatically – as we had done throughout the war – we ducked under the bed, leaving the poor bridegroom stranded.

Peggy Hunter

And forgot to do what we all did in Hong Kong – put a mattress on top of the patient! They just went under the bed!

Drummond Hunter

Once all the excitement was over, up we rose and the ceremony continued. One of our guests was the Royal Scots' colonel's wife and she said, 'I'm going to get you a cake.' So she dashed along the corridors and, of course, in true British style, everything was there – Christmas lunch, Christmas cake, everything. A Royal Scots sergeant was about to cut the cake but she whisked it away and she said, 'I want this. There's a wedding

Peggy and Drummond
Hunter – married as
the Japanese overran
Hong Kong
(Mr and Mrs Hunter)

along there'. And that was our wedding cake! The colonel had ordered all
the booze to be poured down the sink once it was clear the Japanese
were taking over. But he saved a bottle of champagne and we had that as
well. So that was our wedding.

Peggy Hunter

At 3.30 p.m. Hong Kong surrendered. Peggy and Drummond's
bizarre wedding was followed by an even more bizarre honeymoon
– three and a half years in separate Japanese PoW camps.

I used to regret not being able to show our children any wedding
photographs. But, apart from that . . .

Peggy Hunter

We had to start without a single wedding gift – apart from the cake and
the bottle of champagne. I don't regret it at all. Things that happen
unplanned like that can be lasting.

Drummond Hunter

CHAPTER 12

Mad Dogs and Scotsmen

Mad dogs and Englishmen go out in the midday sun.
The Japanese don't care to, the Chinese wouldn't dare to.
At twelve noon, the natives swoon and no other work is done.
But mad dogs and Englishmen go out in the midday sun

Noel Coward, 1932

When the Japanese invaded Malaya in 1941, there were more Englishmen drinking cocktails in Raffles Hotel in Singapore than fighting under the midday sun.

It's hard to believe, but they were having dances, balls and wedding anniversaries down in Singapore, and boys were getting killed maybe thirty or forty miles up the road.

Jockie Bell, Argyll and Sutherland Highlanders, Renfrew

In 1939, the Argyll and Sutherland Highlanders were posted to Singapore and sent up-country to Malaya for gruelling jungle warfare training. There were already Jocks in Singapore: since 1937, the Gordon Highlanders had been the island's garrison.

I always wanted to join the army and went along and joined at sixteen. Why the Gordons? I think it was the idea of going to the Far East – the adventure of it. It was something new and strange rather than staying at home.

Iain MacKenzie, Gordon Highlanders, Stirling

I didn't like it at all, too warm and too smelly. It was rumoured there were twenty-five different smells in Singapore alone. And the heat, the steaming heat – it was wicked. I didn't like the tropics. As a matter of fact, I haven't been abroad since.

Jockie Bell

Iain MacKenzie joined the Gordon Highlanders at the age of 16 (Iain MacKenzie)

OPPOSITE: 'The Argylls sent for me. I didn't want to wear a kilt – not being a teuchter. I'm a city guy' – Jockie Bell (Jockie Bell)

The war seemed far away from Singapore. But the arrival of the Argylls livened things up.

The 'Jungle Beasts' meet the locals
(Imperial War Museum)

We used to fight one another. All the rest were paid on a Friday, but we were paid on a Wednesday so we wouldn't fight with them.

Finlay MacLachlan, Argyll and Sutherland Highlanders, High Bonnybridge

The Union Jack Club: that's where all the battling took place – the John Wayne stuff. It was good! But we were seldom in Singapore – we were out in the jungle most of the time. We got the nickname of the 'jungle beasts'.

Duncan Ferguson, Argyll and Sutherland Highlanders, Falkirk

We were doing training when all the rest were in bed. Mad dogs and Englishmen – they went to bed in the afternoon between two and four. The Argylls were out doing training.

Finlay MacLachlan

We wore khaki shirts and the 'empire-building' hats – the topees. We finished work at twelve because it was thought that the white man couldn't work in the afternoon in that heat.

Iain McKenzie

I think we were the only regiment in Malaya that was prepared for the Japs – the only ones who'd ever done any serious jungle training. Our colonel, Ian Stewart, insisted that all we officers went in among the ranks carrying packs and rifles and doing all the training. He transferred some to staff jobs in Singapore as he regarded they weren't quite suitable for jungle warfare.

Ballantyne Hendry, Argyll and Sutherland Highlanders, Edinburgh

Stewart told them the way the Japs would attack Singapore and they said, 'No, that's impossible, they can't come that way.' It was through swamps, you see; but that's the way the Japs did come.

Duncan Ferguson

As First Lord of the Admiralty, Churchill had been responsible for Singapore's defences. He told the Cabinet:

The Argylls train up-country
(Imperial War Museum)

Singapore is a fortress armed with five 15-inch guns and garrisoned by nearly 20,000 men. It could only be taken after a siege by an army of at least 50,000 men . . . As Singapore is as far from Japan as Southampton is from New York . . . it is not considered possible that the Japanese, who are a prudent people, would embark on such a mad enterprise.

British Cabinet Records, 1940

I didn't give the Japanese threat an awful lot of thought. I didn't think it would happen. I was too busy swimming in the garrison pool. When we heard of the Japanese landing, we rushed to get maps to identify these names. Where were these places? Then we thought, well, they're still hundreds and hundreds of miles away.

Archie Black, Gordon Highlanders, Gretna

Singapore is still to be reckoned with. The gateway to the East is Britain's key point in this war, as the Japs will discover to their cost.

News from Malaya, **Pathe News, December 1941**

On 8 December 1941, at the same time as the attack on Pearl Harbor, the Japanese invaded Malaya. Two hours after the landing, Singapore was blitzed.

We never thought for a minute that Singapore would fall – never for a minute. There were two 15-inch guns pointing out to sea. We didn't know at that time that they couldn't be turned round and fire inland.

Norman Catto, Gordon Highlanders, Scone

It was an impregnable fortress – that's what it was bummed up to be. You could have taken Singapore with a troop of boy scouts with snowballs.

Duncan Ferguson

(*Daily Record*)

What! None Under The Counter!

Up in the Malayan jungle, the Argylls were coming into contact with the Japanese.

The Japs came over with aeroplanes and bombed and machine-gunned us and we never saw a British aeroplane in all that time. Never.

Jockie Bell

Playing their part in the defence of Malaya are Brewster Buffaloes – handy American fighters flown by pilots from Britain, Australia and New Zealand. We have America to thank for these fine aircraft which are a great contribution to the strength of the RAF in this area.

Air Defence of Malaya, **British Movietone News, 1941**

We did see some Brewster Buffaloes, but you could have passed a Brewster Buffalo on a bicycle.

Duncan Ferguson

People tell you the Jap was a great jungle-fighter. He wasn't any better than anybody else. We were ill-equipped. You can't fight with rifles against tanks.

Jockie Bell

As the Argylls were forced back through the jungle, Ballantyne Hendry was dispatched with an urgent message for the Divisional Commander in Singapore.

I went into the mess and they were busy having a cocktail party, and they weren't very pleased when I demanded that I should have some food for my driver. I took him into the officers mess and they were less than pleased. That was their attitude. They had no idea what was going on. We were in contact with the Japs. Fifty miles down the road they were having a cocktail party.

Ballantyne Hendry

For three weeks the Argylls fought a series of almost daily battles as the Japanese advanced 170 miles down Malaya's Grik Road. There was a major battle at Slim River.

That was a massacre. That was the first time they really used the tanks on us. The big-wigs said that tanks could not be used in the jungle but the Japs just came on through the jungle paths. This wee officer – he wasn't an Argyll – came up to me and gave me an anti-tank rifle. He said, 'Take up a position and watch for the tanks coming round the corner.' And I said, 'You must be joking – if you want to fire that at the tanks, you can do it, but I'm not.' You would be just as well with a peashooter.

Duncan Ferguson

It's a terrible thing when you're in a retreating army. You trundle down the road and somebody gets wounded and you and another mate have to carry him between you. If it gets too hot you've got to drop him and run yourself, because it's self-preservation.

Jockie Bell

We met Aussies. They were shouting, 'Don't worry, we'll turn them back.' They didn't realise how bad it really was.

Finlay MacLachlan

I was fourteen days in the bush before I came out and went down to the villages looking for food. The people there gave us away to the Japs.

Jockie Bell

Of 390 Argylls in action, only 90 reached Singapore, but they marched across the causeway from Malaya playing the pipes.

The Australians were defending the shore positions. They must have thought we were crazy playing the pipes. It seemed like we were winning the war.

Tom McGregor, Argyll and Sutherland Highlanders, Stirling

Then they blew up the causeway. But they made a mess of it, so it was no bother for the Japanese to bridge the gap with a couple of planks and get their tanks across.

Finlay MacLachlan

The Japs hit us with everything. They were going to do the maximum damage they could in the time that was left to us.

Iain McKenzie

A belated and tragic last gamble had been made to save Singapore.

There was a full division landed just days before capitulation. Now these men were just sent to their deaths. They knew that Singapore had no chance and yet they still insisted in sending those 20,000 men onto the island to put their hands up.

Duncan Ferguson

They had captured our water supply – the water for the whole city. They were bombing the city ad lib. There was no opposition and the city was an absolute shambles. Conditions in the city were so appalling that General Percival agreed to surrender on 15 February 1942.

Moubray Burnett, Gordon Highlanders, New Machar

The Japanese troops were actually outnumbered three to one and had only enough ammunition to last a few more hours. But they bluffed Percival, through a renewed assault, to capitulate unconditionally. Never in the history of the British Army had such a large force laid down its arms to an enemy. Britain's power in the Far East had been wiped out in ten weeks.

Sunday morning was a beautiful morning. Everything was so quiet, you couldn't hear a bird or nothing. It was the stillness that got to me first. And it was then I was told the war was over. At first I felt happy: 'Oh, I'm still alive.' But then you realised that the Japanese had beaten us and we were prisoners.

Tom McGregor

This still from a Japanese film shows British officers surrendering to the Japanese, 15 February 1942 (Imperial War Museum)

Then I wondered, 'What the hell is going to happen to us?' Because we'd heard so many stories about the Japanese. How they weren't the kindest of individuals.

Iain McKenzie

Who was it went through Alexandra hospital and bayoneted all the doctors and patients? Who was it that raped all the nurses? Who was it that marched the nurses out into the sea and shot them all?

Duncan Ferguson

They always said they would never be prisoners-of-war. They would die for their Emperor. I don't think they could understand why we all surrendered.

Norman Catto

I think the Japs were surprised because they'd captured so many people. And I got a shock when I'd a right look at the Japs. Is that what the hell beat us? Raggedy shirts and rubber boots. What the hell are we letting them beat us for?

Iain McKenzie

I was disgusted. Little fellows! Most of them wore glasses. I just said, 'God Almighty, surrendering to them!'

Norman Catto

A tatty little Japanese came up and told us to drop our arms. And the feeling of despair and shame that one should be defeated by what we saw there was all-consuming.

Moubray Burnett

The defeated now faced another ordeal: three and a half years as prisoners of the Japanese.

'*Banzai!*' – the Japanese Empire has triumphed over the British (Imperial War Museum)

The possibility of Singapore having no landward defences no more entered into my mind than that of a battleship being launched without a bottom.

Winston Churchill, *The Second World War,* **Volume IV, 1951**

And then one became rather angry that so many of us should suffer in the end because of the hierarchy, who mismanaged and misled.

Moubray Burnett

CHAPTER 13

Five Years Without a Banana

I was passionately fond of bananas and we were still getting fruit up until December 1940. We needed ships for troops and munitions, so no more fruit was to come from abroad. I didn't see another banana again for years! It was very sad.

Elizabeth Anderson, Lochwinnoch

We had a chap across the landing from us who was in the Merchant Navy and he brought back a hand of bananas. His mother, very kindly, kept a couple for us and I always remember my sister, who'd never seen a banana before, was so frightened, she started to cry.

Bob Crampsey, Glasgow

In April 1941 British shipping losses were so heavy that Churchill banned publication of the figures for fear of affecting morale. The Government imposed stricter rationing, controlled by the Ministry of Food – 'the biggest shop in the world'.

Yes, we have no bananas! Actress Dorothy Paul reconstructs her mother's sheep's-heid broth for *Scotland's War*. 'She never told us what was in it till we had finished the lot!' (Scottish Television)

I was the office junior and the boss would say: 'Alison, there's a queue in such-and-such a shop in Princes Street. Here's some money. Go and get whatever it is.'

Alison Dunlop, Edinburgh

Queues would gather on a whim. The butcher was getting liver in today, and all of a sudden there would be twenty people outside the shop, even people who didn't like liver. You would cut throats to get the most inedible things.

Bob Crampsey

You made up all kinds of weird and wonderful dishes with weird and wonderful ingredients – cakes with no flour, no fat, no sugar. And you got a lump of stodge out of the oven and that was a cake.

Chris MacKay, Edinburgh

When you went to the cinema you saw a 'Food Flash' which told you 63 interesting ways to use last week's cod and how it was really a tremendous boost that meat – which had been killing us all these years – was rationed. And that the blacker the bread got, the better it was for us!

Bob Crampsey

That's your lot!
One person's rations
for a week
(Imperial War Museum)

The customer would come in and she presented her ration book. The coupons allowed her four ounces of bacon, eight ounces of sugar, two ounces of butter, four ounces of margarine, four ounces of cooking fat, three ounces of sweets and two ounces of tea.

Andrew Nicol, grocer, Tullibody

When you think of it now and you see what we had for a week. One wonders how we survived. But it was adequate and basically it was nourishing. I don't think any of our fathers knew that there were sweet coupons – the first thing you did with a new ration book was rip his out!

Chris MacKay

There was stuff that was allocated, but not rationed, like canned fruit and vegetables. If they were scarce they went 'under the counter' and if they were really scarce, they went 'black market'. If a customer was a regular, they were allocated 'under the counter' goods on their buying power. Rightly or wrongly!

Andrew Nicol

We would queue up at the fishmonger and you just hoped that you would get there in time before the lot that they had in vanished. Maybe the woman six down from you got a pound of haddock, but when it came to you there was nothing left. Well, you thought, she should only have got half a pound and left some for the rest of us. So, there was a bit of friction when it came to queuing.

Bette Stivens, Edinburgh

There were always problems with the people who weren't getting. Loyal customers, who were depositing their ration book with us, they were looked after. But anybody who was coming in just to buy the stuff they couldn't get elsewhere, we didn't look too favourably on.

Andrew Nicol

Everybody cheated. There was always a person or a little shop where we could get a wee bit extra. We were lucky in that my people came from the Western Isles and the odd hen or lump of butter came down.

Chris MacKay

If you had a certain number of hens, you could sell your eggs freely without going through the Ministry of Food. Orkney was really 'egg island'. Everybody used to say, 'The poor souls in the south are only getting one a month.' They knew it was a round thing, but they very seldom saw one!

Walter Leask, Orkney

We had a pet pig called Willie. It was a lovely animal. We used to call, 'Willie', and it came running up to the gate. And during the war we just killed him and ate him. Everyone had a piece. It was lovely!

Jean Mitchell, Blairgowrie

We had, as many a Glaswegian did, a back green which had never seen the plough since the seventeenth century. We had a share of this green which was the size of an average fireside rug. We sowed it with lettuce which grew black, shrivelled and useless. But my brother had sown some turnip seed and he grew a magnificent turnip. You would never have believed that from such unpromising soil such a turnip could come. We had a meeting on how we would eat this turnip and what special occasion we would reserve it for. And someone stole it!

Bob Crampsey

The Ministry of Food kept a check on farmers.

Dig for victory! Scots
were encouraged to
grow their own food
(Roy Smith)

(Imperial War Museum)

Come and help with the
VICTORY HARVEST

You are needed in the fields!

APPLY TO NEAREST EMPLOYMENT EXCHANGE FOR LEAFLET & ENROLMENT FORM
OR WRITE DIRECT TO THE DEPARTMENT OF AGRICULTURE FOR SCOTLAND
15 GROSVENOR STREET, EDINBURGH.

You had officials coming from all directions. I think everyone was in control of it but me. We had the misfortune to be convenient to a tramway line and every official that wanted to get out of the office jumped on a tram to see me!

Lou Anderson, Lochwinnoch

They were usually people who hadn't many scruples. We called them 'snoopers' and it was written all over their face.

Elizabeth Anderson

As well as feeding his own family, Lou Anderson had extra workers helping with his harvest.

These young people have an appetite second to a horse. This wee drop in the bottom of a plate is just not on. The sort of rations that were given out may have been sufficient if you were sitting in an office chair all day, but not if you were wheeling a dung barrow!

Lou Anderson

I used to go up to City Halls in Glasgow to plead for more rations. But, no, that was it. How do you feed sixteen people with two ounces of this and a little bit of Spam? It was in desperation that Lou started bumping off sheep.

Elizabeth Anderson

Food rationing mainly triumphed over large-scale black marketeering. But many of the public weren't always prepared to Make Do and Mend, and a new national stereotype was created.

In the criminal classes there is a love of adventure, a love of cocking a snout at society, applying their brains – they're usually clever. Spivs! They'll always come to the surface whenever there's a crisis. And you also have to recognise that the general public profited from the existence of the spivs – people who knew where to go for scarce items and could market them. So, you'll never eradicate that, never!

Mae MacIntosh, Glasgow

I used to have clothing coupons for myself and two children. I didn't need to buy clothes, I went to the second-hand markets; so what do you think I did with my coupons? I sold them to them that had the money.

Margaret Docherty, Glasgow

We needed extra coupons for our wedding outfits and you only got them twice a year. Now we had planned to get married in December and hadn't enough. There was a man and a woman who stood in Nicolson Square, and on a Saturday you would just say to them, 'Coupons?' And they'd say, 'Yes.' They'd only sell you four at a time. They were half a crown each, so that was like ten shillings for four. I needed eighteen for a wedding dress and twenty-six for his suit. So by the time you'd bought your coupons and paid for your goods as well, it was very, very expensive.

Alison Dunlop

When nylons started, there was quite a black market in them. Anybody that was out training in Canada or the States usually came back with a load. And if you knew somebody . . . who knew somebody else . . . you got a pair of nylons!

Elizabeth Anderson

The Pioneer Corps camped next to my farm. There was a noise in the barn and I looked in and there was an auction sale going on. They were selling semmits, pants and socks. Where they got them, I don't know, but they were just in that day and they had a sale going that night!

Lou Anderson

Hard-won wedding
outfits
(Mr and Mrs Dunlop)

During the war there was no rubber because it was all used for military purposes. Almost everybody wore braces and to have braces with no elastic was a great trial to a working man. Now petrol was rationed, and petrol was very important to my dad. One day he stopped at the local pump to get his last few coupons' worth of petrol and he said to the chap, 'How are you off for braces?' And this chap said, 'I haven't had a decent pair for years.' And my father said, 'I might be able to help you there. I've got two or three good pairs in the shop. How are you off for petrol?' So a little deal was done. I thought this was a great laugh. I used to say to father afterwards, 'Are you going down to put a couple of pairs of braces in the car?'

Walter Gordon, Glasgow

Even fashion served the war effort. By late in the war, four-fifths of new clothes were 'Utility' garments.

Men couldn't have turn-ups on their trousers, ladies couldn't have pleats – because you were only allowed a certain amount of cloth. The Utility mark was CC41 – Civilian Clothing 1941; even underwear had labels with CC41. It was a good thing because quality was controlled and prices were pegged so you couldn't be overcharged for them. Even if you went into some of the posh shops, or into Woolworth's or Marks, it was the same price you paid.

Chris MacKay

'Make Do and Mend': the Government's exhortation to fashion-conscious young women (Roy Smith)

British postwomen call their trousers 'Camerons' and here's the reason why . . .'

The Highland Postie, **Ministry of Information Film, 1943**

'The Camerons have come': Jean Cameron won the right for female posties to have trousers as part of their uniform (Jean Mitchell)

My mother was the postmistress in Glen Clova and the Post Office wanted me to wear a uniform – a skirt and a jacket – and I asked if I could wear my own trousers. It was pretty windy up in the Glen and it wasn't much fun cycling with a skirt. Eventually they said I could have an issue of Post Office trousers – which they then called 'Camerons' – and they asked me to make a film. It was really super fun. I was nineteen and a bit naive. If I'd been fat and forty, I don't think they would have done it! I had so many letters, I sometimes had the mailbag all to myself. I even got a proposal of marriage! One letter was from a lady who was quite offended that I should wear trousers. She said I was a hussy and quoted the Bible at me!

Jean Cameron

While fashion was important to Scottish women, drink was important to Scottish men.

My father had a pub and his whisky quota from a distiller might be six bottles per month. Virtually every Glasgow pub had about two or three non-whisky nights a week when there was no whisky sold *at all!* There was whisky but it was being exported to the United States. Whisky was our great currency.

Bob Crampsey

There were thousands and thousands of cases of whisky in Princes Dock going over to America and the dockers, as any normal person would, tried to get a drink because it wasn't available in the pubs. Some cases were broached – opened and a bottle taken out – and they would drink it between them. Some tried to get whisky out of the docks but the bulge was very pronounced. It was mostly consumed in the docks and we couldn't arrest them when it was inside them!

Alexander Bogue, policeman, Glasgow

Some of the most famous golf clubs in Scotland were down to one tot of whisky per member, per day, two at the weekend. War's hell when it gets to that stage!

Bob Crampsey

When the war ended in the summer of 1945, rationing did not.

Peace was a disappointment as it always is. If anything, the rationing got tighter. You had another eight years of it to go through. I don't think people could have faced it if they'd known that. They were tired of all the restrictions. But overall one's recollections of rationing, for all its human imperfections, are that it was a remarkably fair system. And for all its gaps, we had a better-balanced, healthier diet than before the war in the 'hungry thirties'.

Bob Crampsey

The war is over – but the queues go on: Glasgow shoppers on VJ Day (*Herald/Times*)

Compared to Europe we weren't really all that bad. We were bombed, we were rationed, but a friend of mine in Holland remembers eating daffodil bulbs. Life wasn't exotic but we were never in that state, never starving. But I wouldn't like to go through it again.

Chris MacKay

CHAPTER 14

Every Night Something Awful

When the war started, you had announcements on the radio: 'All cinemas, theatres and places of entertainment will be closed.' For the benefit of the dumber amongst us, they explained that bombs might be dropped and these would hurt people! But after two or three weeks they realised that there was more danger in the population getting bored so it would be better keeping the cinemas and theatres open.

Bob Crampsey, Glasgow

I went down to Govan one dark, wet night and when I arrived there were two queues. Suddenly the sirens went, but nobody budged. There they were in the rain having to wait possibly an hour and half and there was the possibility of an air-raid and they would rather stay there. It showed something of the fascination of the cinema and the desperate need for entertainment.

George Singleton, cinema owner, Glasgow

For those few hours, you went in, and 'to hell with Hitler'. You had a good time.

Jimmy Logan, Helensburgh

To feed the hunger for entertainment, the Government set up ENSA, the Entertainments National Service Association, nicknamed 'Every Night Something Awful' by the forces and factory workers.

There were a lot of people who joined ENSA who had not really earned a living in the theatre before and now they had a captive audience. There were those who could entertain, and there were those who could have maybe entertained a bit better!

Jimmy Logan

ENSA had stars, exempt from national service, who worked for minimal or no fees.

People like Will Fyffe did their pantomimes in Glasgow, at the Alhambra, and went away most of the rest of the year entertaining the troops abroad. Everyone worked seven days doing troop shows in all sorts of wee halls — any place where you could hang your hat up, you went on and did a show.

Jimmy Logan

You'd say, 'Could you tell me where the ladies' is?' And the sergeant would say, 'Yes, follow me.' And a few yards from where everyone was dressing, there'd be a curtain hung up — and, of course, it was a bucket!

Bunty MacLeod, Tiller Girl, Aberdeen

They went on there to entertain an audience that was desperate for a bit of joy. They went on and they did their job. Sometimes people said, 'They're not up to much.' Well, that's their view: I think the boys were glad to see them.

Jimmy Logan

At air-force bases we'd start with a full house and then you'd suddenly see half of them getting up and leaving. They'd all gone off on their raids.

Bunty MacLeod

When ENSA wasn't around, the forces entertained themselves. Norman MacLeod's father had performed with Harry Lauder.

'Stars in Battledress!' A soldiers' amateur jazz band entertain their fellow troops (*Herald/Times*)

MAIN PHOTOGRAPH: Not so Awful? Troops enjoy the show

You had eighty to a hundred blokes stationed on the side of a hill somewhere with no entertainment, so you'd form a little show. My brother and I were in the same unit and we knew gags our father had done. So Johnny played piano and clarinet and I played guitar and we sang songs. We did a terrible act and we called it 'Mac 'n' Tosh'! About a year and a half later we were asked to join 'Stars in Battledress'. You became a full-time entertainer, but in the small print you were still a soldier, and, if the balloon went up, it was – 'Tin hats on, pick up your rifles and off you go, lads.'

Norman MacLeod, Brighton

An army of working civilians needed cheering up too.

The Alhambra was a beautiful theatre. As soon as you walked in, the orchestra started up and I would come out in goose-pimples. The atmosphere was electric.

Bunty MacLeod

In the variety theatres we used to see Dave Willis and Jimmy Logan and you could get a good night's entertainment for two or three shillings. Harry Gordon and Will Fyffe were wonderful performers. Harry Gordon was always the Dame in gorgeous clothes; he looked something like Dame Edna Everage does today.

Chris MacKay, Edinburgh

Bunty MacLeod is Harry Gordon's daughter.

Will Fyffe entertains
Seaforth Highlanders
in North Africa,
3 July 1943
(Imperial War Museum)

'The oldest hen in the Wrens' – alias Harry Gordon (Bunty MacLeod)

Father's great forte was as a female impersonator. During the war he used to do songs like *I'm the Oldest Hen in the Wrens*. One year he said, 'I'm doing a new act in the panto. I'm doing a Land Girl.' And he said, 'Everybody who's seen it so far says that it's your double.' And I thought, 'Oh well, it must be quite smart.' He sent me this photograph of him and it says 'Daddy's Double' on it. When I saw it I was furious and at the same time I had to laugh because it was *so awful!*

Bunty MacLeod

Most entertainers adapted their acts to include patriotic jokes and songs.

In my wee gas-mask, I'm working out a plan
And all the kiddies think that I'm just a bogey man.
The girls all smile, 'cause they can quickly see
The nicest-looking warden in the ARP.
When I run helter-skelter, listen to my cry
An aeroplane, an aeroplane, away way up a kye.
I run helter-skelter and don't run after me
You'll no' get in my shelter, 'cause it's far too wee.

Dave Willis song, c.1943

Jack Anthony was a very good comedian who appeared in the Pavilion. His great forte was to ask people in the audience to shout out the names of regiments. Somebody would shout out 'The 51st Division' which Scotland had a great patriotic empathy for. Jack Anthony would pretend to think for a minute and then say:

Out in the desert, the heat's terrific and the dust obscures
    your vision.
It's only the dust of Rommel's troops being chased by the
    51st Division.'

Hurrah! . . . Tremendous cheering!

Bob Crampsey

The news came over that we'd liberated Paris. So I wrote this wee song which my mother and father used in the show the next night:

You can hear the bagpipes playing across the River Seine.
You can see the kilties swaying, for the boys are back again.
We have liberated Paris and all Frenchmen now are free.
But the 51st won't stop until they're inside Germany.

LEFT: 'Daddy's double'
(Bunty MacLeod)

RIGHT: Dave Willis: 'The
nicest–looking warden
in the ARP'
(*Herald/Times*)

BOTTOM: The Logan
family, with Jimmy on
the left
(Jimmy Logan)

It might sound corny now, and maybe it was, but the audiences loved it.

Jimmy Logan

Ballroom-dancing was the main thing for young people, no doubt about that. And it carried on extensively during the war. Every hall was packed and there were about eighty of them in Glasgow alone.

Farquhar MacRae, manager of the Berkeley Ballroom, Glasgow

The Plaza in Eglinton Street was the one the best dancers went to. The people who weren't essentially ballroom-dancers – who just wanted to shuffle around – went to the Locarno in Sauchiehall Street. The people round the Gallowgate went to Barrowland where they had comedy bands and you laughed all night. The ones who liked to listen to the big bands went to Green's Playhouse. There was a place for them all. And that's where you met your future wife. That's where I met mine!

Manni Ferri, band leader, Glasgow

Even during the bombing it continued. On the night of the Clydebank Blitz the bombs were falling and I could hear them from inside the ballroom, but everybody kept on dancing. It was quite busy that night.

Farquhar MacRae

The NAAFI-cum-dance hall at Adam Sharp's RAF station (Adam Sharp)

I joined up when I was eighteen and I was most fortunate. My initial training was near Blackpool and the first place we made for was the famous Tower Ballroom. When the training was finished we were posted to a bomber station miles from anywhere. My ability to teach dancing was very welcome there. I did my work on the bombers, of course, but in the NAAFI in the evening we ran dances and dance classes for the Waafs and they were most popular.

Adam Sharp, Aberdeen

We went to the Palais in Fountainbridge. On a Thursday night you could get in for sixpence, so that's the night we chose. The Americans were there and if they danced more with you than our own boys, our boys used to get angry and there were always fights.

Alison Dunlop, Edinburgh

You used to go to the dances and all the GIs would get up and you'd think, 'What *are* they doing?' Legs would be flying and they would be tumbling around. And you thought, 'I wonder if I could do that?' With that music you just had to try.

Bunty MacLeod

The Americans were great jivers. I used to go to the Playhouse. I loved jiving. I'm only five foot and I met a big black GI. He was tall and slim and about double my height and I was sure he would end up a professional dancer. I had the time of my life with him. Then two white Yanks started getting on to me for dancing with him. We'd never heard of this kind of thing in Glasgow. I can tell you, there was a right royal stramash – the blooming cheek of them telling me I couldn't dance with a bloke because he was black.

Agnes McLean, Glasgow

While dancing flourished, Scottish football was restricted during the war.

Certain sides, like Aberdeen or Dundee, closed down for the duration or played in a different league. Due to wartime travel restrictions they couldn't come south to play. Players weren't allowed to be full-time professionals. All contracts were cancelled. You couldn't make more than two pounds a week legitimately, so you had to get a job in munitions or join the forces.

Bob Crampsey

There was a lad I knew and he said, 'Are you looking for work, Malcolm?' 'Oh aye, I suppose I will be.' So the next thing was, he got me a job: a capstan and turret lathe operator.

Malcolm MacDonald, Celtic player, Ardrossan

The guy next door was the head of a squad in the boatyard and he said, 'I'll give you a temporary job to keep you going.' So I went in as a temporary worker and stayed there for the rest of the war.

Jimmy Smith, Rangers player, Glasgow

There was a considerable amount of informality about matches. Occasionally, clubs – Hamilton Academical were always doing this –

would arrive two men short. They'd get two men from the terracing and, embarrassingly, sometimes they were the best two players they had.

Bob Crampsey

Malcolm MacDonald and Jimmy Smith played in wartime Scotland *v* England matches.

They were morale-boosters, that's all they were. They weren't true internationals. I remember 1941, I got the biggest showing up in my life. A fellow called Stanley Matthews played outside right. I wish I'd been on the subs' bench that day. That would have suited me down to the ground.

Malcolm MacDonald

I'd every confidence we'd beat them, because we'd beaten them already. But we didn't strike it right. I was just running and the ball wasn't getting there and Matthews was causing a bit of havoc in our defence.

Jimmy Smith

Wembley, 4 October 1941 – final score: England 2, Scotland 0.

Jimmy Smith meets Churchill at the Scotland v England international, 4 October 1941 (Jimmy Smith)

We were beaten five, six, seven and eight nothing during the war by England. We claimed that this was because all the Scottish internationals were needed in the jungle in Burma, fighting the Japs, while the English were swanning round Aldershot. But that doesn't stand up to any examination at all!

Bob Crampsey

CHAPTER 15

Miracle Behind Barbed Wire

One retired North-east farmer is a veteran of the North African Campaign of 1942.

I was in the reconnaissance company of the 21st Panzer Division. All my soldiering was finished when I was taken prisoner. That was the first time I saw a man in a kilt. I got a shock!

Erich Penno, formerly of Königsberg, Germany, now of Keith

The Highland Division takes Axis prisoners in North Africa
(Imperial War Museum)

Throughout the war, Scotland played jailer to thousands of German and Italian prisoners-of-war. By 1943 nearly 40,000 Italians, captured in North Africa, were at work on British farms.

I remember the very first time I saw them. The place was shrouded in freezing fog. The Italians came out with their overcoats, wrapped up, and their caps pulled down over their ears. I can still hear them saying, 'Jesu Christo, bloody Scotland, freezing.'

Reg Clarke, Laurencekirk

In January 1942, one thousand Italians were sent to Orkney. Churchill had ordered impregnable barriers to be built between the islands that ringed the Home Fleet's haven in Scapa Flow. The remoteness and harsh conditions made a workforce hard to find; Italian prisoners were the answer.

The Italian PoWs improved their bleak nissen hut camp on Lamb Holm island with little gardens and a concrete sculpture of St George and the Dragon by Domenico Chiocchetti (Orkney Islands Council)

Lamb Holm Island belonged to my father and he gave it to the army during the war because it had a quarry on it. Part of the barrier was built from the stone in this quarry. The prisoners lived on this island. They'd come from North Africa so Orkney must have seemed the back of beyond to them, especially during the winter months.

Alison Sutherland-Graeme, Orkney

There wasn't any sunshine and everything was damp. There wasn't a tree or a house in sight – it was like being in a desert. You can imagine what it was like for us coming from Italy. There was just nothing there.

Domenico Chiocchetti, Moena, Italy

Our first impressions were dreadful. There were only nissen huts, where we slept – no streets, nothing. In the end, life became bearable. We created a kitchen, a church. The only thing that never improved was the weather!

Vittorio Fabbi, Spoleto, Italy

We were living in terrible conditions, far away from our own families for several years. We lived in a small community, but this created a bond of friendship between us.

Bruno Fugazzola, Varese, Italy

I knew it was my duty to do some useful work for the country where I was held captive. And so, considering everything, I was all right. I didn't suffer physical hardship or hunger.

Remigio Travanute, Trieste, Italy

At first it was very difficult, but we resigned ourselves to living like that. We all prayed that it would end soon. I did six years, six months, eight days and eleven hours.

Pietro Pinesci, Asolo, Italy

In North Africa they made a selection of prisoners who were skilled in certain trades – like cement workers, metal workers, mechanics and drillers. We were allocated numbers and transferred from Suez through Liverpool, Edinburgh and Aberdeen to Lamb Holm.

Bruno Volpi, Cavriglia, Italy

It was a prohibited zone, out of bounds to civilians. The only human contact we had was with our guards. The work on the barriers was very exhausting; there were two squads with different shifts and each team worked an eight-hour shift. They were making cement blocks, so it was very heavy work.

Domenico Chiocchetti

The prisoners came to believe that their work was a breach of the Geneva Convention.

We went on strike because we knew that Scapa Flow was the most important British naval base and we were convinced that this was military work – a defence structure. And so we refused to do this work, as was our right. We received the standard punishment: bread and water for two or three days. Eventually the Swiss Consul came up from Edinburgh and explained to us that the work had been planned for many years but had not been carried out because of high labour costs.

Bruno Fugazzola

They tried to persuade the Italians they were making a road for the benefit of the farmers. But the Italians saw through them. It wasn't really that at all. Perhaps the bread and water diet made them change their minds! So they continued the work and we were very thankful for the road.

Sandy Wylie, Orkney

I saw the Italians working on the wire
across the causeways and in the quarries
with picks and shovels. They were quite
good workers in their way. I remember
two of them tried to escape. Somehow
they got an atlas from Kirkwall and then
set off into the North Sea in a small boat.
I think they gave themselves up. They were
quite relieved to be back!

Sandy Wylie

The prisoners struggled to make camp life bearable. There was a pasta-making squad, a football team, an orchestra and a theatre company.

We had a chaplain who was crazy about the theatre. He had the texts of plays sent out from Italy. We painted scenery and in the evening put on little plays with musicians and actors in costume.

Bruno Fugazzola

The only contact we had with the prisoners was when they put on plays or operas. They came to ask us for flowers and in the evening we were very amused to see the bunch of flowers used in a wedding, then a christening scene and finally at the death bed of one of the actors.

Alison Sutherland-Graeme

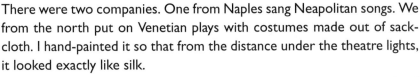

There were two companies. One from Naples sang Neapolitan songs. We from the north put on Venetian plays with costumes made out of sack-cloth. I hand-painted it so that from the distance under the theatre lights, it looked exactly like silk.

Domenico Chiocchetti

The Italians are always artistic. They just can't help being so. They used to make gardens round their huts and little fountains. I think that so many of them were so far away from home that they liked to feel they had brought a bit of their home with them. And then Domenico, who was an artist, asked if they could use one of the huts for a chapel and he started painting.

Alison Sutherland-Graeme

Finding inspiration wasn't difficult. I had in my pocket a tiny picture, which my mother had given me, of the Madonna and Child. I developed the idea and, thinking of our churches here, I decided: 'Let's make a cathedral, not just a church!'

Domenico Chiocchetti

We found material on the blockships – metal, brass, wood, tiles – whatever could be useful. To make the façade, every prisoner coming back to the camp carried a pocketful of cement, a little sand or stones. Everyone took part.

Pietro Pinesci

TOP: The PoW first XI: they beat the camp guards. Bruno Fugazzola is in the back row, third from the left (Bruno Fugazzola)

BELOW: A Venetian play with costumes and scenery by Domenico; Bruno is in the centre (Bruno Fugazzola)

OPPOSITE: Number Two Churchill Barrier seen from Lamb Holm. The cables carry rubble and concrete blocks to the end of the nearby completed causeway. The First World War blockships in the foreground were stripped of material to build a chapel (Orkney Islands Council)

The prisoners and the
chapel façade, with
Domenico standing at
the far left
(Domenico Chiocchetti)

A sympathetic camp commandant, Major Buckland, allowed
Domenico to work full-time on the chapel.

I worked on the chapel for about three years. It was a very different type
of work for me! I began with the altarpiece of the Madonna and Child,
then I worked on by hand bit by bit painting the walls. We had a
blacksmith and a carpenter, but they could only work outside their
working hours. It helped me to pass the time and I forgot about the
horrors of war.

Domenico Chiocchetti

I always remember that when they were going away from the island and
the buses were at the end of the barrier, my father and I went to see them
off. Some of them were in tears. I think Italians are emotional, but it
showed that they can't have been altogether unhappy in Orkney.

Alison Sutherland-Graeme

When I'd finished the work and left it behind, I was very sad. In fact, I
wrote a letter to the Orcadians saying: 'I'm so sorry to have to leave the
chapel, but I'm leaving you a piece of my heart.'

Domenico Chiocchetti

It is one of the good things that war has brought. Whenever we look at
the chapel, we can be thankful to all those men who built it and left it to
Orkney to look after.

Alison Sutherland-Graeme

We created this and left it to the Orcadians and to Scotland. Nobody likes war and my chapel is a symbol of peace. To everyone – of whatever nation – I say: 'Come, see what we prisoners made. It is a testimony to peace.'

Domenico Chiocchetti

Orkney was a unique case. In most camps life was easier.

The Italians were easy-going to the point of being lazy. They weren't really keen on working. They were very friendly with everyone, particularly the girls. One or two actually married local girls. The Germans were a totally different lot. They were very smart, very keen to work. No back-chat, no lazing about. Nice lads.

Reg Clark, Laurencekirk

I joined the Waffen SS. It was a Panzer élite force, something similar to the Marines or the Commandos. In 1942 I saw service in Russia and in 1944 I was put to the 10th Panzer Division in Normandy. On 10 July, the Scots regiments tried to take 'Hill 112'. I was blown out of the turret of my tank and, after six days lying in a field, was captured.

Werner Busse, formerly of Halberstadt, Germany, now of Inverness

The chapel's altar with Domenico's fresco of the Madonna and Child. The 'stonework' is painted plasterboard (Domenico Chiocchetti)

When I was fighting in Africa, I didn't think about going home again. I thought more about when I would be killed because I knew I wouldn't get out alive. I was captured and taken to America as a prisoner-of-war. People used to come and stare at us to see what Nazis looked like.

Erich Penno

We were assured by the Americans that we were going to be repatriated. But in Liverpool they took us off the ship and sent us to Scotland, to a camp near Cragellachie.

Werner Busse

At the end of the war there was a desperate shortage of agriculture labour in Britain, and German prisoners went to work alongside civilians on Scottish farms.

People were mostly very friendly towards us. I met a family in Buckie. Two of their sons had been killed in action, but these people bore us no hostility. I suppose they felt we were young boys and felt sorry for us. That opened my eyes to Scottish hospitality.

Werner Busse

Werner Busse in the uniform of the Waffen SS (Werner Busse)

Erich Penno, the young soldier of the 21st Panzer Division (Erich Penno)

Aberdeenshire was all right to work in. But Morayshire was the place no prisoner wanted to go to. They weren't treated as humans there.

Erich Penno

British intelligence officers came round and sorted out people from the East – the Russian zone. And they told us it would not be advisable to go back there because the Russians would take us into custody.

Werner Busse

After you were released from the camp and you had stayed for five years, you could change your job. But by that time I was at home in the farming world. I had met Margaret, whose father I worked for, and we decided to get married.

Erich Penno

There was a barn dance and I must admit I was a wee bit drunk that night. I saw my future wife and I said, 'That's the girl for me.' At our wedding in Brechin, my father-in-law said, 'I fought against the Germans in the First World War. But better my daughter marries a good German than a bad Scotsman.'

Werner Busse

Erich and Margaret Penno farmed near Keith for forty years. Erich has developed a broad Buchan accent.

I'm Scots. When I go abroad I use my Scots tongue. If they don't understand me, they'll have to find an interpreter. All my bairns and my grandbairns, they're Scots through and through.

Erich Penno

Deep down I'm still a German. But I made a good choice, a very good choice, adopting Scotland as my second home. I've spent seventeen years in Inverness and I've only once seen any hostility. In my job as a bar manager I was a disciplinarian. If I barred anybody, they sometimes called me a Nazi. But that's the only time.

Werner Busse

Margaret Stewart marries her father's German PoW farmworker (Mr and Mrs Penno)

CHAPTER 16

Revenge on Rommel

Rommel was held in very high regard by friend and foe alike. I think we had a very healthy respect for his ability as a general. We very much wanted to turn the tables on him.

Hugh Robertson, Seaforth Highlanders, Glasgow

Rommel had respected the achievements of the 51st Highland Division in France despite the odds against them. Having been captured at Saint Valery in 1940 and then to kick him out of Africa was very satisfactory indeed.

Ian Robertson, Seaforth Highlanders, Nairn

The 51st Highland Division, Scotland's most high-profile fighting unit, had risen from the ashes of Saint Valery.

I was adjutant at Fort George in 1940 when the first 51st was captured. It was decided that the 9th Scottish would change its title to the 51st Highland Division and reform as that. All the regiments came from the same districts as the original division. We were lucky in getting General Douglas Wimberley as our divisional commander. He was a great traditionalist and was determined that the Highland Division would be as Highland as could be.

Ian Robertson

I was told I would be General Wimberley's piper. There were three conditions: (a) I was to be a reasonable piper, (b) I had to speak Gaelic, and (c) it would be a bonus if I were able to read and write it.

Angus MacDonald, Cameron Highlanders, North Uist

He would go to almost any lengths to get Scotsmen into the Division. If they'd been wounded and were fit to come back, he would move heaven and earth to get them, rather than Englishmen.

George Dunn, Royal Scots Fusiliers, Arbroath

He was lovingly called Big Tam by the men. But they felt he was over-anxious to get the Highland Division involved all the time – in absolutely every battle.

Donald Robertson, Seaforth Highlanders, Inverness

The Desert Fox, Africa 1942
(Imperial War Museum)

I mind a time when we did think, 'Why should *we* be off again? Why the 51st again?'

Jock More, Seaforth Highlanders,
Wick

Wimberley's Division was to be one of five infantry divisions of General Montgomery's 8th Army up against Rommel's Afrika Korps. The Desert Fox had been made Hitler's youngest Field Marshal when he took Tobruk in June 1942.

Big Tam and Monty
inspect a
guard of Gordon
Highlanders, 1942
(Imperial War Museum)

The first job we did when we landed in Suez was to make a fire of all the topees – the sun helmets we were issued with in the UK. A couple of days later we were all wearing tam o' shanters – the proper Highland dress.

David MacGough, Black Watch, Glenrothes

We were moved to a camp at the base of the pyramids and then it was a question of training for desert warfare. We had to get acclimatised to having sand in our stew, sand everywhere else, and living in the desert.

Angus MacDonald

The food was mainly bully beef and hard biscuits. There was some sweet potatoes but I didn't much care for them. And there were flies everywhere!

Willie Galleitch, Seaforth Highlanders, Inverness

There was a terrible lot of dysentery and there were boils. Boils on the back of your head, on your arms, on your legs. It was really horrible.

John Horn, Middlesex Regiment, Edinburgh

Edinburgh-born John Horn was with an English regiment.

I said I'd like to go to the Black Watch, but unfortunately I got posted to the Middlesex Regiment. Luckily we were amalgamated with the 51st Highland Division as their support regiment for machine-guns. You hear about animosity between the Scots and the English; well, that never happened, I can assure you. Not between the Middlesex and the 51st.

John Horn

In August 1942 the 8th Army was strung along a forty-mile line due south from the Mediterranean – Alexandria and Cairo's last line of defence. In front of them were almost half a million mines and Rommel's Afrika Korps. Montgomery's first task was to boost morale.

He visited all the troops and spoke to them with such confidence about what was going to happen that people felt that here in North Africa was a turning-point in the war.

Ian Robertson

Monty came round before the actual battle started. He distributed cigarettes to everybody and made a morale-boosting speech. We were always kept well informed. This was something that Montgomery insisted upon. Everybody, down to the lowest ranks, should know what was going on.

John Horn

Finally, when it came to the attack at El Alamein, Monty saw that the Highland Division was put in between two very experienced divisions, the New Zealand Division and the 9th Australian Division. So we were put into battle on the right foot.

Ian Robertson

Ian Robertson, as Highland as could be (General Robertson)

The coming of the dawn over the Mediterranean. The sunset with a touch of green. Many soldiers saw these things, perhaps for the first time, and they wrote their letters home or smoked and talked, or lay silent and listened to the pipes as they played 'Highland Laddie'.

***Desert Victory*, cinema documentary, 1943**

We spent the whole of 23 October in holes in the ground. We weren't allowed to emerge from our little slit trenches because we would have been revealed to the other side.

George Dunn

Everyone was afraid. Anyone who tells you they don't experience fear is not being truthful. If you're a sergeant or a platoon or company commander, you have so much preparation to do before the battle commences that you haven't really time to think of yourself. What you are thinking of mostly, are the men under your command. But the infantry soldier has much more time to think. There is nothing to take their mind off what may be before them. There's fear all round you. There's fear in the air above you. There's fear in the ground beneath you. There's shelling above you and mines in the ground underfoot.

Donald Robertson

You could hear a pin drop before the guns opened up.

Hugh Robertson

It was a terrific barrage and it was still going on the next day. It was deafening, with the big guns at the back, and the medium guns in the middle. You wonder how anything existed there.

David MacGough

We were protecting the start-line and the Black Watch came through us. And all we had to distinguish ourselves from the enemy was to wear St Andrew's crosses on our haversacks. And when you've got several hundred men of the Black Watch coming up behind you, some of them rather trigger-happy, it's quite frightening.

Donald Robertson

We formed up to attack through the German minefields. We had advanced four thousand yards behind a creeping barrage. We were told that we must stay very close to the barrage and I think we got far too close. We'd only gone a few hundred yards when my platoon sergeant was wounded.

Hugh Robertson

The trouble was that one was inclined to go too fast, and when this happened you ran into your own artillery shells. We did have one or two casualties that way.

Willie Galleitch

I counted the number of men I had at that stage – and I had eleven men left in my platoon. I'd started with twenty-one, so it didn't look too good.

Hugh Robertson

The number of pipers that lost their lives during the first night of El Alamein was quite colossal. The Argylls in particular suffered very badly. They had one of their bands virtually wiped out. Then the powers-that-be realised that if this continued they would have no pipers left in the division. After all, it takes about seven years to train a piper and seven generations before that to make a good one.

Angus MacDonald

I think the pipers were something we should have saved and savoured for other times. They could have played us from the start-line, but I think it was foolhardy to send them, without weapons, leading the men into battle.

Donald Robertson

We all knew that there were going to be casualties. But when you see a convoy of ambulances passing you for the first time, it really does sink in very solidly that this is real war. It's no longer toy soldiers playing at exercises. You're liable to get it at any time.

Angus MacDonald

I came across a lieutenant in the 5th/7th Gordons – a fine-looking man. And there he was, lying by the desert track, dying. His life's blood ebbing away. Believe you me, I found it very stressful and very sorrowful.

Donald Robertson

The other two platoon commanders were killed. The company commander was in a bren carrier which went over a mine. He lost his foot and died the following day. So I was the sole surviving officer of C Company. It was quite a thought.

Hugh Robertson

When you checked up on the number of casualties among your men – the number of dead, the number of wounded – it was then that you thought, 'Could I have done this better and saved some of these lives?' That's always the worrying thing.

Donald Robertson

The battle lasted ten days and nights. Allied losses were 13,500, but half of Rommel's army – 50,000 men – had been killed or captured. The Desert Fox was on the run, but fought a series of brilliant rearguard actions.

After Alamein, the big push started after the retreating Germans. I remember the first night we stopped I was standing with a few Jocks around me and suddenly we got shelled. Everybody was shouting to take cover. I

MAIN PHOTOGRAPH: Piper MacDonald of the Seaforth Highlanders leads Jocks in the desert (Imperial War Museum)

INSET: Highland Division pipers suffered colossal losses at El Alamein (Imperial War Museum)

don't remember anything more and it was only in daylight the following morning that I looked down at my boots and saw they were covered in pieces of flesh and blood. The Jocks must have just been blown up.

John Horn

The pursuit of Rommel's army was to last seven bloody months. Over the two-thousand mile chase to Tunis, the Highland Division left their mark.

We were always putting 'HD' signs up. We got a reputation for it. We were known not as the Highland Division, but as the Highway Decorators. At Tripoli there was very great competition about who got there first. We claimed we got in first and the 7th Armoured Division claimed they did.

George Dunn

The General made sure that the 'HD' slogan appeared before anyone else's. Those who thought they were first into the square at Tripoli found a big 'HD' already there. They were none too pleased.

Angus MacDonald

The 'Highway Decorators' paint a house in Sfax, Tunisia, April 1943 (Imperial War Museum)

On the massive Axis defensive line at Mareth in Tunisia and later at Wadi Akarit, the Allies met determined opposition from the outnumbered Afrika Korps.

For all the experiences we had from Alamein, right through to the end of the European campaign, most of the Highland Division would agree that Wadi Akarit was one of the worst. We had a terrific amount of casualties. We had to go over the top. It was about three or four hundred feet up and rock-face all the way and the Germans were firing at us. You couldn't dig in anywhere. We were just lying on the top without any cover. I remember eventually getting into a slit trench and walking up and down thinking, something's wrong here, this is soft for a slit trench. It wasn't until dawn approached that I realised I was walking over dead Italians.

John Horn

The Germans were excellent fighters and very well trained. They would fight till the bitter end. They wouldn't give up without a struggle. I thought they were excellent. Almost as good as we were.

Donald Robertson

Rommel was a legend and he led these two or three formations of Germans very well, but he was out-numbered and out-generalled in the end.

George Dunn

Rommel left Africa forever in March 1943, an exhausted and sick man. The Afrika Korps held out for two more months. It was the first major Allied victory of the war and was celebrated with a big parade in Tunis, led by the pipe bands of the Highland Division.

Once the battle commences, the generals' plans go for nothing. Winning the battle depends entirely on the 'other ranks' and it is they who get maimed and die in their hundreds. They are the people who do the suffering, they are the poor chaps who go out there and go forward without question to fight and die. One must not forget the very, very great part the 'other ranks' play in any war. One must never forget that.

Donald Robertson

Graves of Seaforths who fell at Wadi Akarit in April 1943
(Imperial War Museum)

Sunset on an Atlantic
convoy: the 'Wolf Packs'
attacked at night
(Imperial War Museum)

CHAPTER 17

Those in Peril

Naval ratings used to look down on us. I remember one time a naval rating said, 'Medals – what do you guys get them for?'

Archie Smith, Merchant Navy, Glasgow

We know what we did. I'm not sure whether other people knew. But then they must, because otherwise they would have starved.

Jim Paterson, Merchant Navy, Durham

To keep Britain's lifelines open, more than 32,000 merchant seamen – every one a volunteer – died. The Merchant Navy casualty rate was equal to that of some of the most daring front-line forces.

I was on the regular Atlantic crossings with the *Cameronia*. We arrived on the Clyde on Friday, 1 September 1939, and the *Athenia* was going downriver, outward bound to Canada. We passed on the river and she was sunk on the Sunday morning war was declared, 3 September. We sailed back out to New York again on 5 September, without a convoy or an escort. We were terrified of being torpedoed and when we got to New York there was quite a feeling of revolt that we weren't going to be escorted home again.

Archie Smith

The *Athenia* was the first of almost three thousand Allied merchant ships sunk by German U-Boats. British ships were equipped to defend themselves and merchant seamen trained as gun-crews.

You had to pass your test as a gunner and you had three or four naval gunners along with you. We used to do a lot of shooting in Barra before the war – rabbits and wild birds – so I was pretty good with a gun.

Lachlan MacKinnon, Paisley

Hebrideans had a tradition of service in the Merchant Navy. Many were also in the Royal Naval Volunteer Reserve and were called up at the outbreak of war.

We joined the *California* in Glasgow and headed for Scapa Flow. It was an armed merchant cruiser – an AMC. We called them Admiralty Made Coffins, because they were being sunk all over the place!

Billy MacLean, Isle of Lewis

In the Battle of the Atlantic, Hitler tried to starve his one surviving enemy. To keep food and weapons flowing in, Britain adopted the tactic of the convoy.

You had to go to Halifax, Nova Scotia. All the ships heading into the Atlantic massed there to get into the convoy.

Lachlan McKinnon

The harbour there – the Bedford basin – could take all the ships in the world, I think. There were huge transatlantic liners and ships heavily laden with stuff from the States – tanks and aeroplanes – and they were low in the water. And our cruiser was huge, so it looked like a duck with her ducklings coming after her.

Billy MacLean

U-Boat commanders –
like the fighter-pilots of
the First World War –
were German national
heroes
(Imperial War Museum)

It was quite fascinating to see how a convoy was composed, with the troopships right in the centre and well protected, the cargo ships in another ring, and the escorts and the destroyers on the outer ring. You could see a black flag going up and you knew there was a submarine alert – and you'd hear depth charges. But being right in the centre of the convoy you felt *quite* safe.

Archie Smith

On one trip, we left from Halifax with 76 ships in the convoy and we ended up with 122. It was the largest convoy that ever crossed the Atlantic. We could only do seven knots – the speed of the slowest – zigzagging all the time, to mislead the submarines.

Billy MacLean

From late 1940, U-Boats began attacking convoys in 'wolf packs' – groups of eight or nine striking together at night, on the surface. Jack Woodburn survived the attack on Convoy HG76 in December 1941.

Every night we were attacked. We know now that four submarines were sunk, but our big aircraft carrier, the *Audacity*, was sunk. And the *Stanley* went up in a very, very bright flame and lost a great many men.

Jack Woodburn, ship's engineer, Ayr

We were depth-charging all the time. And when we were asleep down below, it sounded very eerie. You could hear the bangs in the distance.

Billy MacLean

I heard the second mate come rushing along the deck saying, 'There's a submarine on the starboard side.' We saw the wake of one torpedo going down the starboard side and one torpedo going down the port side. And we were sandwiched between the two. The submarine crash-dived. The captain thought we had sunk it, but I knew we hadn't. I opened up the engines as much as I could. We were getting more frightened of our engine than what was outside, because we had 2,500 tonnes of high explosives aboard!

Jack Woodburn

We tried to rescue the survivors who were in the water. But we had to get off our mark as fast as we could. If you stopped at all, you were very vulnerable. You could have unfriendly submarines coming round, firing things at you. Just to encourage you to move on.

Jim Paterson

The war at sea ranges over the oceans of the world. Our warships are now escorting convoys to Russia. And in our unstinting admiration of Russia's heroic fight, let us not forget the men of our convoys who are as much in the battle of Russia as the Russians themselves!

***Supplies to Russia Get Through*, British Movietone News, 1942**

If you didn't get to the survivors in the Arctic in a few hours, they were finished. Especially if they were soaking wet when they went into the lifeboat. They could be frozen.

Murdo Smith, Royal Navy, Isle of Lewis

We were going through white fog for about an hour. When we came out of it, even the wireless aerials were over three inches in diameter. The whole ship was frozen.

Billy MacLean

Defending the convoy was difficult in the freezing fog. You couldn't see a thing until you saw the torpedo bombers coming at you out of the cloud. You only had a few seconds to aim.

Murdo Smith

I saw this plane coming and I said to myself, 'I can get you.' And I started firing into her – but she was still coming at me. And I said to myself,

Survivors of a
U-Boat attack are
plucked from the
Atlantic
(Imperial War Museum)

Frozen signaller on board HMS *Sheffield* on an Arctic convoy, 1941 (Imperial War Museum)

'You're daring enough. This is getting too close for comfort. She's going to land on our deck.' If she had landed on our deck, that was us away! We were carrying one hundred octane fuel. But then she just went 'plunk' into the water beside us.

Lachlan McKinnon

There were 36,000 Merchant Navy men killed during the war. We had sixty-five ships in the Clan Line before the war and there were thirty-five of them sunk, or mined, or torpedoed. With a great loss of life. And here am I – I've never even got my feet wet. I was very fortunate.

Jack Woodburn

The 'Lewis boys' on the *California*; Billy MacLean is in the second row, second from the right (Billy MacLean)

Barra suffered a great loss of life for a small, remote island. I lost my brother.

Lachlan McKinnon

There were forty-two in the crew of the *California* from Lewis and we were allowed to have a church service every Sunday night. And at home they used to have prayers every morning and every evening for us. We believe that had something to do with

us getting home. All the Lewis boys on that ship came home after the war.

Billy MacLean

This is the diary of P.H. Franklin, 3rd Radio Officer of MV *Richmond Castle*, a fruit ship of eight thousand gross tonnes. Everything was very quiet and peaceful when suddenly, like a bolt out of the blue, the ship gave a sickening lurch and there was a terrific blast – we had collected a 'tin-fish' just aft of the engine-room.

Peter Franklin's Diary, 4 August 1942

The mother of a Yorkshire wireless operator, Peter Franklin, wishes to thank a Lewis seaman for saving her son's life and the lives of his seventeen companions. The seaman, Angus Murray of South Shawbost, rigged sails on a lifeboat with blankets and oars and sailed her to safety for nine and a half days through high seas.

***Stornoway Gazette*, 2 October 1942**

In 1992 three Englishmen, John Lester, Peter Franklin and Derrick Cutcliffe, travelled to the Isle of Lewis to visit Angus Murray. The four men were last together fifty years previously – for ten days in an open boat in the North Atlantic.

We've been able to get hold of the log of the U-Boat 176 and he had been shadowing us since five o'clock in the morning. We must have gone straight into their hands.

John Lester, Newbury, Berkshire

15:16hrs. Dive. Steamer lies to right of the point of the bow. Attack course, 280 degrees.
15:56hrs. Shoot a three-pronged fan of torpedoes.
16:20hrs. Steamer is under water.

Log of U-Boat 176, 4 August 1942

I heard this terrific thud. It took some seconds to sink in and then this green wall of water came cascading down and I realised what had happened. My first thought was, 'I haven't got a lifejacket.'

John Lester

FROM TOP TO BOTTOM:
John Lester, Peter Franklin, Angus Murray and Derrick Cutcliffe

The silly things you thought of doing. I went to my wardrobe and took a pair of silk stockings I'd bought for my girlfriend. I wore them for a while in the lifeboat because all I had on was a pair of shorts. They kept my legs warm – a bit. But there was a certain amount of leg-pulling over that one.

Derrick Cutcliffe, Bideford, Devon

Surface. There are three fully-occupied rescue-boats and a life-raft. Name of the steamer, *Richmond Castle*.

Log of U-Boat 176

There had been many stories about the atrocities suffered by chaps who'd been torpedoed, being shot-up. And it crossed my mind: 'This is curtains.' The U-Boat came up alongside. They gave us tins of bread and butter, cigarettes and field dressings. They gave us the course and distance to the nearest land and they wished us good luck.

Derrick Cutcliffe

Our lifeboat had lost the oars, the mast, the sails and the water. We had so little we didn't attempt to drink any until the third day.

Peter Franklin, Harewood, Yorkshire

One boat was picked up on the same day as ourselves, miles away. They had three chaps die. The other boat was picked up after six days and they had six men go. It was mainly through what we would now call hypothermia, exposure, fatigue. Had we been much longer, we would have started to have people die as well.

Derrick Cutcliffe

Because you go to sea in a large ship, it doesn't mean that one had any idea at all about how to sail a small boat. We were in the extremely fortunate position of having a Western Islander aboard.

Peter Franklin

5 August. We had on board Able Seaman Angus Murray. This morning I saw that he was busy with two sodden blankets. 'Och, I'm just making a sail,' he said.

Peter Franklin's diary

I had an uncle and I used to go out lobster-fishing with him. He used to direct me and tell me what to do. He would say, 'Now, when you're in a situation like this, this is what you do.'

Angus Murray

Angus was there – calm, cool and collected. He sailed the ship day and night. It sounds an old-fashioned, corny thing to say, but he sailed it by the feel of the wind on his cheek and we travelled five hundred miles in nine days, which, with two blankets, was quite an incredible feat.

Peter Franklin

I can remember seeing waves forty feet high, green and curling at the top, and I thought we would never get through this. My memories of Angus are of him calm and very quiet . . . and he at that time . . . *[breaks down]* . . . I'm sorry about this . . . but I remember it very vividly . . . saved the lot of us. It's a memory I shall never forget. Thank you, Angus.

John Lester

You were between life and death. But I was very confident when I got the sail going and we were running before the wind. It really strengthened my faith in the Lord.

Angus Murray

Angus's skills and composure in the boat, without any doubt, saved the lives of all of us. It was one of the great moments of my life to meet him again and thank him. An absolutely marvellous man!

Derrick Cutcliffe

I can remember someone saying, 'There's a ship' and we all thought it was another U-Boat. Then gradually it came nearer and we saw it was a corvette. An immense feeling of relief suddenly went through all of us.'

John Lester

Soon we were being helped across the decks of the corvette by sailors who absolutely radiated kindness. They gave us food. They gave us their bunks. It still gives me a warm feeling inside whenever I think of them. Now I realise what people mean when they talk of the brotherhood of the sea.

Peter Franklin's diary, 13 August 1942

That submarine was sunk in May 1943 off Cuba, with all hands. They were probably in a worse condition than ourselves. The losses in the German submarine service were practically equal to the Merchant Navy – 33,000 in both. They were fighting just as grim a battle as we were – grimmer. It was their everyday life to make war; it was not ours.

John Lester

A seaman on the corvette *Snowflake* took these photographs of Angus Murray and his friends being rescued. The middle picture shows Angus sitting at the back of the boat on the left; Peter Franklin is on the oar in front of Angus, Derrick Cutcliffe is on the other oar and John Lester is standing at the front of the boat in a white T-shirt (John Lester)

September 5, 1942

PICTURE POST

HULTON'S NATIONAL WEEKLY

In this issue:

DIEPPE: THE FULL STORY

4D

SEPTEMBER 5, 1942

Vol. 16. No. 10

CHAPTER 18

Achtung Achnacarry!

The media took over and spread stories of derring-do. But that was never the reality of the Commandos – the skulduggery, devil-may-care, gangster-warfare kind of thing. That was never the style. Everybody was a volunteer and there was a splendid relationship between officers and men. It was a club, a family, a clan. Yes, clan's the word! And Achnacarry fitted into that concept. It was clan country.

John Gibson, Edinburgh

The Commando Memorial at Spean Bridge dominates the Lochaber landscape and the estate of Achnacarry, Britain's principal training ground for Allied Commandos.

Scotland meant a lot to the Commandos although we were drawn from all over, from Cornwall to Shetland. The west Highlands served the British Army well in starting off this idea of really arduous infantry training. So although no enemy set foot in the Highlands and although they might seem remote from London and suffered very little from blitzes, they played an important part in the war.

John Gibson

After Dunkirk, Churchill wanted assault troops that could hit back and he entrusted the job first to Lord Lovat and Lovat's cousin, Bill Stirling.

Donald Gilchrist, Ayr

Lovat and Stirling began training men for unconventional warfare in remote estates throughout Lochaber. Their work spawned the SAS, the Special Boat Squadron and the Commandos. Formal Commando training was eventually centred at Achnacarry estate, the ancestral home of the Camerons of Lochiel.

OPPOSITE:
A wounded Commando, the hero of a press account of Dieppe (Hulton-Deutsch)

Nissen huts sprouted in the grounds of Achnacarry House as the Commando instructors prepared to train men for battle; Commanding Officer Charles Vaughan is seated in the centre (Jack Rowley)

I think the army chose it because they wanted a place that was in the protected zone, north of the Caledonian Canal. It was easy to get at by rail to Spean Bridge but it was remote and could be sealed off. It had ideal training ground with lochs, rivers and hills. My father accepted that it was very suitable for them and passed the estate over.

Sir Donald Cameron of Lochiel

I was absolutely determined to join the Commandos. People today don't realise that this was a war where the values were black versus white. Today it's two muddy shades of grey. So I had no doubt. My problem was could I get in?

Ronnie Williamson, Edinburgh

I was fed up. My father had lost a lung during the First World War at the hands of the Germans. My parents were being bombed in Manchester where we lived. My career had been halted and I thought the only thing to do is to get involved – and in a very pragmatic way: kill people.

Harry Sullivan, Macclesfield, Cheshire

My father had been a signal sergeant in the Cameron Highlanders at the Battle of Loos. I grew up with legends of laying cables under shot and shell. So I joined the Royal Corps of Signals at Glasgow University OTC, but found quite quickly that signalling was a matter of intricacies with wireless sets and I was absolutely no good at it. Volunteering for the Commandos was the only way to get back into the kind of war in which I felt I might do something.

John Gibson

One of the instructors senior to me couldn't understand why a young chap like me was not trying to get into the action. He came back with a newspaper which showed some Commandos back from a raid, their black faces all smiling. And he jabbed his finger at the picture and said: 'That's what you should be in.' So, being stupid, I applied!

Donald Gilchrist

Ronnie Williamson:
'Could I get in?'
(Ronnie Williamson)

You were brought into a room with a forty-watt bulb hanging from the ceiling and it's the middle of winter. There are four officers there, a medical officer, a major, a captain and a lieutenant. But they're not sitting facing you. They're all round about you and the first thing you've got to do is strip. Then you get a medical examination and a cross-examination simultaneously. And the whole object of the operation is to try and disorientate you.

Ronnie Williamson

I was dressed in my Cameronian uniform – my tartan trousers, my belt shining and so on. But they all seemed quite disgusted with the display.

Donald Gilchrist

The medical officer was saying, 'Now stand on one leg. Take a deep breath,' and immediately the major comes forward and says, 'Why do you want to die so young?' At the end of twenty minutes you don't know what to expect and when I turned round I discovered that they were all smiling. I didn't know they *could* smile and then they said, 'Congratulations, Williamson, you're just the kind of man we want.' The relief was enormous!

Ronnie Williamson

Four, five hundred miles on a train to Achnacarry, non-stop. No food, and for water we had to get snow off the top of the carriage. Through the night in a blacked-out train, arriving at Spean Bridge without any briefing. That was horrendous. With about 60 pounds of gear we dropped onto the rails. If ankles were broken, you were put straight onto the train again. The instructors were on the other side of the platform and they were so fit they were running up and down bristling with energy like butchers' bulldogs. They were raring to get at us, and they did! And then we had to march the seven or eight miles uphill across moorland, up 'Heartbreak Hill', as it was called, and you were piped into Commando Centre.

Harry Sullivan

On your arrival at the front gate there was this amazing sight: a whole row of dummy graves. The crosses read: 'This man put a bomb down the mortar the wrong way' . . . 'This man trod on his climbing rope' . . . 'This man advanced over cover.' You knew you were in for a very hard time.

Ronnie Williamson

The commanding officer at Achnacarry was Colonel Charles Vaughan. Donald Gilchrist was his adjutant.

Vaughan reckoned that Hitler didn't stop the war because it was Sunday, so the training went on every day. He also reckoned that Hitler didn't halt the war because it was raining or snowing. When the trainees first came up it was raining – coming down in buckets. They would huddle wherever they could get shelter, thinking, 'Oh, they'll call off the training and we can go to the NAAFI and drink tea.' The next minute there was bawling and shouting and there they were doing drill with the rain pouring down, or going off to the assault course, or into the hills.

Donald Gilchrist

Charles Vaughan
(centre) and Donald
Gilchrist (right)
(Donald Gilchrist)

Achnacarry was a crucible, in a very inhospitable part of the Highlands. The Nevis range was all around with snow on the tops. When it wasn't bitterly cold it was bitterly cold and raining. We had all types of training, designed to make the commitment you had into an efficient commitment and a willingness to kill. They started off by frightening you so that you learned to live with fear.

Harry Sullivan

The training was tough. Vaughan had evolved assault courses like the 'Death Ride' and the 'Tarzan Course' which ran along the trees beside the River Arkaig, a network of ropes on which we tried to emulate Tarzan.

Donald Gilchrist

Seven drowned on one occasion. We had a Death Ride which they used to slide across at full speed. The rope broke and they fell into the river. We used to throw bombs at them as they were going across. They were blown off and they landed in the river. They weren't able to make it. One had to be able to swim.

Niall Thomson, Commando instructor, Tain

One of the most difficult things, in bad weather, was the thirty-six-hour scheme – about a hundred men out on the mountains for thirty-six hours. It rained from the moment we started until it finished. We had to band together to get over the hills in the wind and the sleet. Sometimes you took two paces forward and one pace back. It was dreadful. You went to sleep soaked, cold. But if you're tired enough, you'll sleep. And we were up very early in the morning, stamping our feet to get warm. And it was off to make a mock attack down near Achnacarry.

Donald Gilchrist

You learned camouflage and how to live off the land. One time they were cooking and this sergeant said, 'How would you like to sample this?' I said, 'What's that?' 'Oh, it's a piece of crow.' The next one would be a piece of rat. But that's living off the land!

Danny Davidson, Coatbridge

Unarmed combat sounds horrible now, but I and most of my friends felt that we and our families were going to be killed. Our way of life was going to be totally destroyed. So when people taught me how to disable a man with a knife, I didn't rear back in horror. You know: how to cut his tendons, how to cut his throat, how to stop thinking you didn't kill a sitting target – and how to welcome a sitting target. If the fellow was sitting with his back to you, you were in luck.

Harry Sullivan

The object was to create as little disturbance as possible. Do the job efficiently and disappear. So the fighting knife was adopted as the emblem of the Commandos.

Niall Thomson

Oh, Loch Lochy at night! That stayed in my memory. Lot of whizz-bangs going off and charging onto the shore. After drill on Catterick parade-ground, it felt like getting into the real thing.

John Gibson

As they paddled towards the shore Very lights went up into the sky which lit up the scene and there was a crash of tracer bullets right over their heads. As they got near the landing-ground there were instructors throwing live grenades into the water which caused explosions, and three-inch mortars which caused huge spouts of water. And as they landed and started to run towards their target, demolitions went off throwing up peat and mud. It was a Hollywood scene.

Donald Gilchrist

Commando instructor Niall Thomson at the right of the back row (Niall Thomson)

All the exercises were done with live ammunition. And there was quite a number killed at Achnacarry. I think it was forty or forty-one men. The object was to make it as realistic as possible, as near wartime conditions as possible, and I think we succeeded in this. I'm quite sure there were a lot of lives saved as a result. We were putting people into battle. We had to make sure they lived, so the harder we trained them, the more chance they had of living.

Niall Thomson

If the training was effective it was usually more realistic than the real thing. Certainly it was more demanding and it never let up. You were so exhausted with the training that the real thing came as almost a relief.

Ronnie Williamson

The instructors had an obsession to fit you to kill the Germans. I reckon they would have been very offended if a German had killed you.

Harry Sullivan

Among foreign soldiers trained at Achnacarry were US Rangers.

One American got a ricochet through his buttock. There could have been an international incident – letters from the President of the United States and so on. But when they were going back, there they were – marching, shoulders hunched, soaked, hen-toed like John Wayne. This man who'd been hurt had become a joke: 'Where did ya say he got it, man? Ya don't say? Right in the ass? Sure glad it ain't my ass!'

Donald Gilchrist

Soldiers and sailors who had fled from occupied Europe retrained with the Commandos.

Many of them had had miraculous escapes before reaching this country. And here they were, joining the Commandos, ready to go back. There were some marvellous troops and, of course, if we were going into Holland or France, we would have French or Dutch soldiers with us who knew the language, knew the population. They were very gallant indeed.

Donald Gilchrist

I had a price on my head. We were condemned to death by the Germans. If they had found out that I was in the Free French forces, my family could have been arrested and tortured. I already knew the kind of training because I'd done it in the French Marines. I was really proud to be a Commando, to win the Green Beret.

Raymond Hervo, formerly of Brittany, France, now of Fort William

It's an achievement to throw away your glengarry and put on your Green Beret with the badge on it.

Danny Davidson

He was no longer a soldier. He was a Commando soldier. Quite a difference!

Niall Thomson

It sounded dangerous to be in the Commandos. But actually you were probably a lot safer because you had people around you who could react instantly – at a moment's notice – to anything that happened.

Ronnie Williamson

Gerry doesn't like these blokes. He doesn't know when they're coming, or where.

***Commandos Raid Again*, British Movietone News, 1942**

I went to No.4 Commando just in time for the Dieppe raid in August 1942. We were lucky. From our point of view, it was almost a copybook bid led by Lovat which went round the sides and got behind the German guns. The thing I particularly remember was Lovat standing up amongst us and waving his hand at the buildings and saying, 'Set them alight. Burn the lot.' And I thought, 'Well, this is not a colonel of the British Army. This is a Highland chieftain bent on the total destruction of the enemy.' But the Dieppe raid was remembered as a disaster because the Canadian troops went into a cauldron of fire. They were subjected to great losses. But I like to think that these men were not lost for nothing. I believe that many of the lessons that came from the Dieppe landing saved a lot of lives in the D-Day operations.

Donald Gilchrist

During the Second World War, Commandos won 38 battle honours and lost 1,706 men in action. Survivors gather each year on Remembrance Sunday at the Commando Memorial in Lochaber.

TOP: 'Gerry doesn't like these blokes . . .' (British Movietone News)

BOTTOM: Final orders from Lovat, the Highland Chieftain (right) (Imperial War Museum)

Naturally, you think of the people who got lost along the way. But, at the same time, you think of the camaraderie and the friendships in the Commandos. It was a very important period in people's lives.

Ronnie Williamson

I believe that we are now accepted as a family, a clan among the other clans. And it's my hope that, like Finn McCool and his warriors of Glencoe, we too in later years might become a legend in Lochaber.

Donald Gilchrist

Soldiers of the Highland Division wade onto a Sicilian beach: the Allies were back in Europe (Imperial War Museum)

RIGHT: Captured in civilian clothes attempting to get through the Allied lines, a German paratroop officer is questioned by Hamish Henderson (Imperial War Museum)

CHAPTER 19

The D-Day Dodgers

For almost two years, the Allies fought a bitter campaign from the shores of Sicily to the foothills of the Alps.

The idea circulated in Italy that Lady Astor had said in the House of Commons that the troops who had stayed behind in Italy, rather than going to take part in D-Day in France, were D-Day dodgers. And people were singing to the tune of 'Lili Marlene' – 'We are the D-Day Dodgers. Way out in Italy.' My first reaction was, 'This will make a good song.' And I put together some of the fragments to make the song which is now generally sung as 'The D-Day Dodgers'.

Hamish Henderson, Intelligence Corps, Blairgowrie

> We're the D-Day Dodgers out in Italy
> Always on the vino, always on the spree.
> Eighth Army skivers and their tanks
> We go to war in ties like swanks
> For we are the D-Day Dodgers, in sunny Italy.

Nobody failed to experience fear. You come out of a submarine and suddenly feel you're all on your own in the darkness. They bombed the beaches and thirty-two gliders came in overhead and then the moon appeared quite brightly and we paddled in. We knew we were on exactly the right beach and then turned out to sea and shone our torches to the waiting fleet. It meant that four canoes could bring in 3,250 ships by shining torches out to sea.

Ronnie Williamson, Special Boat Squadron, Edinburgh

A handful of British Commandos had launched the first Allied invasion of the enemy's home territory, in Sicily on 9 July 1943. More than 180,000 troops landed along one hundred miles of beach. For the first time since Dunkirk, the Allies were back in Europe in force.

I was very anxious to get ashore, and to set the men an example by being the first off the boat. I leapt off and went right down over my head in the sea. Tremendous laughter. They were quite delighted that their company commander had got soaking wet.

Donald Robertson, Seaforth Highlanders, Inverness

We put the troops ashore and the poor devils were getting mown down. Bombs were dropping, killing a few of them at a time. Landing barges came round the ships to see if we had any dead to take ashore.

Archie Smith, Merchant Navy, Glasgow

We were up against Hermann Göring paratroopers. They were very difficult men. Even if they were lying wounded, they would still fire at you. But they were good soldiers.

David Pryde, KOSB, Ceres, Fife

I was one of the first troops to go into Francofonte. But unfortunately the German paratroopers arrived.

Donald Robertson

I got into an orange grove and started firing machine-guns. It was then that I was wounded for a second time and my namesake, Big Robbie, was also hit by the same shell. He was very badly wounded and lying on the road covered in blood.

Hugh Robertson, Seaforth Highlanders, Glasgow

I got bullet injuries on each side of my torso, one through the side of my neck and then, unfortunately, a shell burst above me and got me in the neck again. I believe that was one of our own mortars.

Donald Robertson

The only way he could get out was on a bren-gun carrier. I eventually got the stretcher onto the carrier and told the driver to go as fast as he could through the gap. Fortunately, Big Robbie made it.

Hugh Robertson

I landed in Sicily as a platoon commander and within three weeks I was commanding the company. It was quite an ordeal when you think that someone, little more than a boy, was responsible for the lives of one hundred plus men.

Jim Drummond, Cameronians, Airdrie

After hard fighting in Sicily, the Allied army crossed the Straits of Messina to Italy.

The Germans had withdrawn from the toe of Reggio Calabria. I remember the Italian women came down on the beaches with bottles of Chianti. They seemed quite pleased to see us. So we couldn't compare this with the landing at Sicily.

Andrew Brown, Argyll and Sutherland Highlanders, Aberdeen

Within days of the landing, on 8 September, Italy announced its surrender. The news cheered a second invasion force bound for Salerno, south of Naples.

They announced the surrender and we thought: 'This is great. We don't have them to worry about.' We had the Germans to worry about though, which was a different story.

Peter Paterson, Royal Scots Greys, Glasgow

By first light we started going in and all hell was let loose: 88mm guns had a go at the landing-craft coming in. We lost five tanks. One officer was killed and two soldiers.

Bill Haynes, Royal Scots Greys, Dalkeith

It was chaotic. Infantrymen running here and there. We were being shelled – not only by the 88mms, but also from the hills. They had a good target – like the coconut shies at the fair.

Len Binks, Royal Scots Grey, West Calder

A mortar dropped beside the tank and a piece of shrapnel got me in the head. And the blood started. I daren't take my earphones off because I thought I'd lost my ear.

Bill Haynes

A planned five-day push from Salerno to Naples took nearly a month. By 10 October, 12,000 Allied soldiers had been killed, wounded or captured.

We landed at Salerno, a holiday with pay
Gerry brought his bands out to cheer us on our way.
Showed us the sights and gave us tea
We all sang songs, the beer was free
For we are the D-Day Dodgers, the lads that D-Day dodged.

As the British/American 5th Army took Naples on the west, Montgomery's 8th Army advanced up the east coast. On both fronts, the Germans had an ally – the landscape.

It is ideal country for the Germans, for the retreating force to defend each mountain, each valley and each river one by one. Tough going. It never stopped raining except when it snowed. Everything was sodden. The Germans blew up every bridge. The infantry crept though this soft fluid mud. If you stood in it too long it came up above your knees. Movement was extremely difficult and it rained and rained all the time. Nasty.

Denis Forman, Argyll and Sutherland Highlanders, Moffat

The winter came in and we moved inland to the mountains of Castel di Sangro and it was supposed to be the worst winter the Italians could remember. We lost sixty people with exposure and six died.

David Pryde

We were three, four, five thousand feet up. It was snowing and freezing cold and we were out on the mountainside. You would have to live it to realise how cold it could be. It's not all sunny Italy!

Jim Drummond

Two views of the war in Italy from a German propaganda leaflet (Imperial War Museum)

We found the native mountain population were fighting the Germans and one of the most fascinating months of my life was organising these partisans into an effective fighting force. My God, they were wonderful at the fieldwork of spotting and shadowing the enemy, garrotting the enemy in twos and threes, sticking knives into the enemy. All of that they did splendidly. But not quite so hot on the set-piece stuff!

Denis Forman

The fighting in the mountains was intended to keep the enemy pinned down on their defensive Gustav Line right across Italy, rather than letting them mass at Monte Cassino which barred the Allied advance to Rome on the east coast.

There had never been anything like Monte Cassino. It was a vertical slab of rock with Germans on top and Germans behind. And on the pinnacle above Cassino town was the Benedictine monastery. Four different attacks, three major ones. All failed except the last one.

Denis Forman

We had a defence establishment at the castle halfway up the hill. The castle – in my humble opinion – was not worth holding. I think if the Germans had been really serious they could have taken it back. It had been captured in the initial attack and prestige said we must hold it.

Hamish Taylor, Argyll and Sutherland Highlanders, Southend, Kintyre

On 15 March 1944 waves of bombers dropped 2,500 tons of bombs to flatten the monastery and Cassino town in preparation for a new assault.

After the bombing we were meant to move up this precipice to get to the top and take the monastery. It wasn't possible. Everyone knew it wasn't possible, but it had been ordained by the High Command that we should do this. I got up to the castle at about seven in the evening. There was a German attack on the castle which got to about forty yards away, but the guys inside kept them at bay. Shells were falling and I saw one drop into a shell hole. I said to my batman, 'Lightning never strikes twice in the same place – we'll go into that shell-hole.' And lightning struck twice instantly. Another shell came out of the

Close combat amid the ruins of Monte Cassino (Imperial War Museum)

Treating the wounded in
an Anzio dugout
(Imperial War Museum)

sky from the New Zealanders and landed on my left leg, which was then smashed. After that, I don't remember a lot. I was taken into the castle and got a good dose of morphia which saw me through the day. I believe my leg was amputated in an Indian medical field station at the foot of the hill.

Denis Forman

Halted at Monte Cassino, the Allies planned a landing at Anzio sixty miles up the Mediterranean coast, just south of Rome. It would, they believed, outflank the Gustav Line, cut its supply routes and drive the Germans from Monte Cassino. But the Allies made a critical mistake and delayed their advance.

I thought they should have carried on from there into Rome. We were pushed back to the beachhead. And it was rough.

Alex Robertson, Royal Scots Fusiliers, Alexandria

It wasn't a pretty picture when we landed because the Germans had had time to consolidate their forces and had started pushing our troops back into the sea.

Norman Smith, Reconnaissance Corps, Isle of Lewis

When we got there in March, we found that there were cooks and signallers and anybody who had a rifle and two legs in the front line. It was a very serious situation.

David Coutts, Royal Scots Fusiliers, Gatehouse of Fleet

There was a little hut – I'll always remember it – and our quartermaster said, 'We'll take this over until the vehicles come ashore.' It was the worst bloody place we could have gone because we were strafed stupid by the Stuka dive-bombers.

Alex Robertson

They had snipers and if anybody put their head up they were whacked. There was a terrible sickly smell of death. This was with us all the time because we couldn't bury anyone. When our men were mown down they had to lie there.

John Wilkie, Cameronians, Hamilton

It's very difficult to understand what it was like living underground for four months. Especially when we knew we were in the range of German artillery all that time and more or less in the front line. It was just a beachhead, after all.

Norman Smith

On 18 May, Monte Cassino fell to a final assault by Polish soldiers. In the five-month Cassino campaign 45,000 men – on both sides – had died. Many bodies were never recovered from the ruins.

The town looked – to me – like the face of the moon. Within five or six miles round Cassino there wasn't a tree, there were just stumps. I remember one little farmhouse on the plain sticking up there like a sore thumb.

David Pryde

By the time of the Allied break-out from Anzio on 23 May, the Germans had lost 10,000 men, the Allies twice that number.

> Palermo and Cassino were taken in our stride,
> We did not go to fight there, we just went for the ride.
> Anzio and Sangro are just names,
> We only went to look for dames,
> For we are the D-Day Dodgers, in sunny Italy.

Cassino and Anzio veterans linked up and headed for Rome.

It seemed to me a terrible thing if we were to enter Rome and there would probably be American bands playing. So I took the initiative and went to see both div. commanders who agreed that the pipers should be put together for a ceremonial parade in Rome. After all, the Scottish troops had done a lot of fighting on the beachhead. So Scotland put up a show in Rome when the city fell, and the Romans loved it. It was only just and fair, if you are months on a beachhead, to have an afternoon of parades.

Hamish Henderson

It was very popular with all the Italians, of course. Thousands of them turned up to hear this. But we hadn't many kilts — just enough to dress our officers and NCOs as we went walkabout. We were quite an attraction in Rome.

Hamish Taylor

MAIN PHOTOGRAPH:
A Roman triumph! Pipers march from the Colosseum, 4 June 1944 (Imperial War Museum)

The kilt, quite an attraction for the signorina (Imperial War Museum)

The Roman triumph was short-lived. Two days later, on 6 June, the Allies invaded Normandy. D-Day made Italy yesterday's news. The D-Day Dodgers felt a forgotten army as they headed north of Florence for another winter in the mountains. The Germans fought on for ten more months, surrendering only a week before Berlin.

What was D-Day? We didn't understand the language. We were much more concerned about where all these D-Day people were on A, B and C days.

David Coutts

Lady Astor, wasn't it? Bloody lassie! She got it entirely wrong because we thought we fought a hard campaign. No disrespect to the D-Day people, but we had to fight on mountains and all the bloody rest of it, in weather like nobody's business. We objected to that 'D-Day Dodgers'!

Alex Robertson

Dear Lady Astor, you think you know a lot,
Standing on a platform and talking bloody rot.
Dear England's sweetheart and her pride
We think your mouth's too bloody wide –
That's from your D-Day Dodgers, way out in Italy.

Look around the hillsides, through the mist and rain,
See the scattered crosses, some that bear no name.
Heartbreak and toil and suffering gone.
The lads beneath, they slumber on.
They are the D-Day Dodgers who'll stay in Italy.

A British stretcher-party
at Monte Cassino
(Imperial War Museum)

CHAPTER 20

A Day at the Beach

D-Day has come. Early this morning, the Allies began the assault on Hitler's European fortress.

BBC Radio News, 6 June 1944

Lord Lovat had formed the 1st Commando Brigade. And he said, 'Millin, you have volunteered to be my piper, and two Scotsmen will spearhead the landings in Normandy at the head of over 300,000 men. I, a Scotsman, and you, a Scottish piper.' And I said, 'Thank you very much, Sir.'

Bill Millin, Commando Piper, Dawlish, Devon

It was New Year of 1944 that we first landed on the Normandy beaches. We did that three times — the night before Hogmanay, Hogmanay, and the night after. They felt that the Germans wouldn't be expecting us at that time of year. There were lots of aerial photographs, but they didn't know the depth of the water or the density of the sand and what weight of vehicles it would take. So that was our job — to find out. We also had to take in the sappers who took samples of the beach and weighed up the various obstacles. They couldn't land without the information we'd got. I was a young lieutenant talking to admirals of the fleet and people who were planning the landings and they said, 'Now, Wild, what do you think?' And they took your word for it. I couldn't believe this but after all I had been there and they hadn't!

Peter Wild, Naval Commando, Kelso

Piper Bill Millin prepares the Commandos to spearhead the invasion (Imperial War Museum)

In 1943 the Clyde was one of the main ports of the invasion build-up. Allied troops poured into Greenock on their way south. The mountains and coastline of Scotland became a vast invasion battle school. Untried troops were specially trained for assault landings in the same tough territory as the Commandos.

George Duncan (front row, centre) with the Assault Platoon of the 1st Battalion KOSBs in September 1943, who were trained to clear mines and obstacles on D-Day (George Duncan)

From 1941 onwards, we trained all the time for landing somewhere. We went to Loch Fyne, Inveraray, and we used to scramble down nets, get into motor-boats and go and land on the assault beaches – so called! – at the head of the loch, and then march back. That was the worst part of it, marching back! And then they discovered that Burghead Bay in Moray was almost the same kind of beach that we'd land on in Normandy. So that was quite exciting – except that in December 1943 you were rather cold, wet and waist-deep in water and carrying all your equipment! When we landed in Normandy they drove us right onto the beach. We had a dry landing. But not at Burghead Bay!

George Duncan, King's Own Scottish Borderers, Edinburgh

I think it was probably as different as night is from day. The only similarity was the fact that there was sea at Normandy as well as Burghead and also sand. But there were no angry men at Burghead Bay!

Vic Campbell, KOSB, Catrine, Ayrshire

All over Scotland, people prepared for the invasion. Mary Cuthbertson built landing craft in the Kelliebank Yard in Alloa.

We'd heard about the build-up and were quite keen to get going, to play our part in it. But, oh dear, the plates buckled and things went wrong. And they seemed so flimsy. We thought, 'Poor soldiers who had to go off in these!'

Mary Cuthbertson, Tillicoultry

I came up to the old Lobnitz yard at Renfrew on the Clyde late in 1943 to stand by an LCF – a landing-craft flak. We sailed it all the way from here and then eventually to the Normandy landings in June. Before the war you used to get on paddle-steamers to sail to Rothesay and Dunoon – never to the beaches of Normandy!

Walter Jennings, Royal Navy, Glasgow

Meanwhile veterans of North Africa and Sicily had been recalled for the invasion of Europe.

We all went home with our Africa Star thinking we were veteran soldiers. The 51st Highland Division had been told by the colonels and generals that we were the best division in the 8th Army and we had to live up to that name.

Bert Mitchell, Gordon Highlanders, Dingwall

In the run-up to D-Day the Gordon Highlanders were stationed at Chalfont St Giles in Buckinghamshire.

The pipe band would beat the retreat on the village green. The locals all turned out and we'd adjourn to the pub and have a few pints.

Jimmy George, Gordon Highlanders, Keith

Jimmy and Molly –
married just before
D-Day
(Mr and Mrs George)

They made a big impression on me. They were very strange because of their accent. They seemed quite like foreigners to us. Then I met Jim in the pub and from then on, he was the one for me.

Molly Blizzard, Chalfont St Giles

We courted for a few months and then we decided we'd get married before D-Day. I managed to get a few days' leave and we got married in the village church.

Jimmy George

Jim just had a few days, then he had to go off to war again.

Molly George

We knew something big was about to happen, but we didn't realise it was imminent until we left Scotland for the South. The place was jam-packed. In all the country roads there were vehicles nose to tail for miles, as far as the eye could see.

James Barclay, KOSB, West Kilbride

It was chock-a-block with soldiers, vehicles, guns. And of course it was all sealed off. Nobody could get in or out. It was like an exclusion zone.

Archie MacLean, Royal Navy, Glasgow

There was one thing that was really drummed into everybody: 'Careless talk costs lives'.

Walter Jennings

MAIN PHOTOGRAPH:
Gordon Highlanders
board their landing-craft
for the assault on
Normandy, 3 June 1944
(Imperial War Museum)

We knew our heads were on the line. If we spilt the beans, we should be the first to cop it. We'd have to tell lies; we'd arrange to take Wrens out that night, never to turn up!

Peter Wild

My fiancée said, 'We'll get married on such-and-such a day'. And it dawned on me that (a) I wouldn't be there, and (b) it was perilously close to D-Day!

Alastair Pearson, CO 8th Parachute Regiment, Gartocharn, Dunbartonshire

Supreme Allied Commander Eisenhower weighed up the weather reports. Just after 4 a.m. on 5 June – with the words 'Okay. Let's go!' – he committed the greatest fleet the world has ever seen to an assault the next day.

A great armada assembled off the Isle of Wight, codename Piccadilly Circus. Six thousand ships and a quarter of a million men.

Donald Gilchrist, Commando, Ayr

There were endless planes flying overhead. The Allied planes had black and white stripes on their wings. They were called the Cab Rank. You knew that if there was any nonsense ahead they were waiting to dive and do their stuff.

George Duncan

'You haven't a clue what it's going to be like': engineers of the Highland Division en route to Bernieres-sur-Mer, Juno Beach, 6 June 1944 (Imperial War Museum)

The Allied air forces flew almost 15,000 sorties that day and dropped 20,000 tons of bombs.

The crossing was fairly rough and when they served up breakfast in the middle of the night, I never saw so many men turn green. Many a man was glad to face the Germans rather than stay on the boat.

John Russell, KOSB, Dundee

We realised we were in for something but we had no idea of what. But there was nothing much we could do about it then. We were very much a captive audience.

Vic Campbell

We were all young – I was only twenty. So we were fairly ignorant of what war was like. You think it's going to be glory when you get there. You haven't a clue what it's going to be like.

John Russell

When you went the first time at Alamein you didn't know what to expect. By this time we all knew what could happen. So we were a bit more apprehensive than the first time.

Bert Mitchell

You're calming your own fears, trying to remember what you were there for and knowing that we would come up against something pretty bloody and awful before very long.

Revd Charles Stuart, Padre, Gordon Highlanders, Banchory

Late on 5 June, Allied airborne troops had boarded their aircraft and gliders.

My advance party dropped at twenty past twelve and the main party dropped at ten minutes to one. I knew quite well that something had happened because instead of the sky being full of parachutes, there were singularly few.

Alastair Pearson

Pearson's 700 men had been too widely scattered over the drop zone. In the dark he tried to gather a fighting force.

Paras prepare to drop behind the German coastal defences, 5 June 1944 (Imperial War Museum)

I had about 170 chaps after about two hours. I planned on getting 50 per cent but I didn't. It wouldn't have been so bad if it had been a balanced fighting force but it wasn't. One of my soldiers loaded his sten gun, pulled the trigger and the bullet went straight into my hand. It was extremely painful.

Alastair Pearson

We arrived about half past five, frightened to death. We were going to be the first people there, literally in front of everybody. Our job was to lead in the Sherman tanks. We had a sign at the back of our boat and they swam behind us until we got them to within twenty-five yards of the beach. We didn't know how soon we would be blasted out of the water, how many mines we might hit. But it worked like a charm.

Peter Wild

Piper Millin (right foreground) leaves the landing-craft at Sword Beach at 7.30 a.m. on 6 June 1944. To Millin's left is Lord Lovat, wading ashore beside a column of his men (Imperial War Museum)

Assault troops poured ashore. Lord Lovat led his Commando clan – Number One Special Service Brigade – across the plain of Normandy. And over the sounds of battle, the scream of shells, the thump of mortars, the rattle of small-arms fire, came the high fluted notes of the pibroch. It's Lovat's piper, with a swagger to his kilt.

Donald Gilchrist

Just after seven thirty the ramps went down and Lovat jumped into the water and I followed him. And when the water was at waist height, I started to play 'Highland Laddie' and, when he heard, he turned and smiled.

Bill Millin

The first thing I saw when the ramp went down was one of these tetrahedron things – an enormous cross of steel sticking out of the water. The water was choppy and this Lieutenant Glass and I were ploughing our way through the water. There was a hell of a scream from him and that was the last I saw of him. But we were told not to stop. There was plenty of back-up coming to collect the wounded. Well there were an awful lot of wounded.

Ken Kennett, Commando, Symington

At the entrance to the road off the beach, there were about ten to twelve wounded British soldiers. Then I heard the noise of a British flail tank coming up from the water's edge to explode the mines. The commander couldn't see them and his tank just came straight on and crushed its way up this narrow road over the top of the soldiers.

Bill Millin

The sad thing was the piles of bodies. There wasn't time to bury them.

Peter Wild

Lovat said, 'Piper, glad to see you. Do you mind giving us a wee tune?' And I found it rather strange that he should ask me to play a tune under those circumstances. But I started marching up and down playing the pipes and this chap came up on my left, the drones' side, and said – I can't use the bad language he did – 'Are you ****** mad?' But I ignored that and kept marching. There were French as well as British Commandos all lying along the beach and they were cheering. So I thought, 'That's only one person who doesn't like bagpipes.' I don't know if he was an Englishman or not!

Bill Millin

Inland, Pearson's paratroopers were trying to protect the bridgehead.

The objectives were to destroy three bridges over the Dives to stop German reinforcements coming in from the east. I had until nine o'clock in the morning to destroy them and they were all destroyed by eight.

Alastair Pearson

Pearson's fiancée Joan was still unaware the wedding was off.

It didn't honestly dawn on her until the morning of D-Day when an old boy she knew asked her if she'd heard the aeroplanes go over last night. She said she hadn't and he said, 'Well you'd better turn on the news, because there'll be no wedding on Tuesday!'

Alastair Pearson

Under the command of General Eisenhower, Allied naval forces, supported by strong air forces began landing Allied armies this morning on the coast of France.

BBC Radio News, 6 June 1944

We heard it on the radio because we always had the radio tuned in for any news of what was happenening. And whenever the planes went over, you used to belt out and watch them and think, 'They're looking after them.' You just wondered what was in store for him and of course it was a while before I heard from him. It was a very worrying time.

Molly George

We wanted to get on with it. We all wanted the war finished. I was quite experienced by this time. You knew what you were going into and you just hoped you'd get through to fight another day.

Jimmy George

It was only within sight of the French coast that you began to wonder what it would be all about, and by then the Germans were firing at us, opening up their big guns.

Revd Charles Stuart

We were listening on the intercom to one of the landing-crafts in distress. 'We're breaking up, we're going.' This was what we heard and then panic: 'We're going, Good luck, lads.'

Alec Wentworth, Royal Artillery, West Kilbride

We kept picking up survivors – about 220. Five died aboard and they were buried at sea before we got into Portsmouth.

Billy MacLean, Royal Navy, Isle of Lewis

The first one that went off just disappeared, it was too deep. He had all his kit on and just disappeared completely.

Bert Mitchell

Craft weren't coming in close enough and the men were getting drowned because they were hitting them before they could get into shallow water.

John Russell

We were as green as grass going in there. There weren't many of the troops that went ashore that day that had battle experience.

Alec Wentworth

We got ashore and I looked out of the side and saw a dead body lying there. That was my first impression. I said to myself, 'What am I doing here?' That was one of my first thoughts. What was I doing here?

James Glennie, Gordon Highlanders, Aberdeen

The training we had simply accustomed us to a way of living. But it was all so terribly different when 6 June dawned – and it stayed different. We were supposed to try to capture Caen that day, but 21st Panzer Division was there and we weren't really expecting them so soon.

Vic Campbell

The 21st Panzers came round and hit us and we heard that first night that there was a chance we were going back into the sea.

John Russell

This is where you stay and fall and die if necessary. We were not to move one inch. You mustn't go back. Forward, do not go back. If you do, that will let the Germans through and they will be able to shell the beaches and destroy anything coming in from the sea. When I look at it now, that was the correct decision. But it isn't very nice to be told: 'Here you stay and here you die.' But that's what had to happen.

Ken Kennett

By nightfall on 6 June, getting ashore and staying ashore seemed like a victory. Nearly ten thousand allied troops were killed, wounded or went missing on D-Day. German casualties have never been established. There were 337 days of war in Europe still to come.

FROM TOP TO BOTTOM: Bert Mitchell, John Russell, Alec Wentworth and James Glennie

Seaforths in a
Normandy field,
25 June 1944
(Imperial War Museum)

CHAPTER 21

News from the Front

To me the actual D-Day stuff is blown up too much, when you think what some of the soldiers suffered after that. You only have to look at the cemeteries in Normandy. Most of these people weren't killed on the beach, they were killed after that.

Ernie Bright, Commando, Glasgow

> The Normandy bridgehead that was won from Hitler's Europe on D-Day was only the first action in a European campaign that lasted nearly a year.

The Germans were only a matter of 200 metres away. You could lie there and watch them and they were lying there and watching you. You were more tensed up then than coming over on the landing-craft. I was more afraid of the German mortar teams sending that mortar over into the Amfreville area. Every night, every morning, you could set your watch with it. They were very good at it. First class.

Ernie Bright

Breville was the worst place I have ever been in at any time during the Second World War. It had been a lovely wee village at one time, but it was blown to pieces. You could smell death all over the place. There was a pond there with two men in it. They had been killed and they were still in the pond. But it was too dangerous to try and get them out because it was sniped all the time by the Germans.

Ken Kennett, Commando, Symington

You heard the gun go off and then you heard the scream of the shell coming in and you had a good idea where it would land. But compared with a mortar – well, you didn't hear them, they just hit the ground and exploded.

Sandy McKenzie, Gordon Highlanders, Fyvie

You were living on your nerves. The first six weeks before I was wounded, I don't suppose I slept any more than half an hour each night.

You couldn't sleep because it was constant shelling.

John Russell, King's Own Scottish Borderers, Dundee

From muddy slit trenches, soldiers sent home news from the front. Molly George was desperate for news of the Scottish soldier she'd married just before D-Day.

I missed him terribly. And you didn't get any information. You weren't supposed to know where they were. And of course the Germans were very good fighters and you knew it wouldn't be easy. Other friends had married soldiers too, and we always asked each other, 'Have you had a letter?'

Molly George, Chalfont St Giles

We came up against a German tank. His gun was swinging round and we didn't really stand a chance because we didn't have anything to fire against a tank. He hit our bren-gun carrier and that went up in flames.

Jimmy George, Gordon Highlanders, Keith

It was such a relief when you got the first letter – to know that he was okay.

Molly George

William Blackhall McPherson, Provost Sergeant of the 5th/7th Gordon Highlanders, wrote a remarkable series of letters from Normandy.

I made a point of visiting the British military cemetery at Hermanville. I watched a French family reverently place some flowers at the foot of the neat, plain little crosses. I asked, 'Did they know any of these dead heroes?' No, they said, it was but a silent appreciation of the men who gave so much in the liberation of their country. I pointed out the grave of a friend of mine and they told me his grave would never lack a fresh flower.

Sergeant William Blackhall McPherson, letter, late June 1944

I knew Willie quite well. I went to school with him. He was in charge of the battalion police and, of course, if anyone stepped out of line he had to deal with them. That made him a little bit unpopular with some people. I never got caught doing anything, so I was all right!

Jimmy George

Sergeant William
Blackhall McPherson
(Miss Blackhall
McPherson)

McPherson's tough military bearing in France belied a gentler side, evident in his letters to his family. He was the youngest of twelve children from a family in Keith, Banffshire. His surviving sister, Betty, and niece, Anne, still treasure his letters.

Willie was the youngest, just a baby when my mother died. Peggy, my oldest sister, was sixteen and she brought us up. Willie was called up in 1940. He liked the army, but he was anxious to get the war over. He was always writing letters to the family, mostly to Peggy.

Betty Blackhall McPherson, Keith

He wrote to me from North Africa and France and sent me postage stamps. He always complained if I didn't write back. My mother got this letter from Willie, when my brother was killed. It says: 'In all this death and destruction, this has been my bitterest moment. And though I cannot help you, I am praying that God will give you the strength and courage to pull through. Do not regret that Bill ever joined the Air Force, but rather remember that it was his choice and as he wanted it. God comfort you all. My dearest sympathy. Willie.' My mother treasured that letter, just as Peggy and Betty treasured theirs.

Anne Davidson, Elgin

Early on D-Day plus 6, the Gordon Highlanders' headquarters at Touffreville was attacked.

The Germans were very naughty. They were shooting up our wounded and the stretcher-bearers who were going out to pick them up, and I felt this was a bit thick. So I did use a rifle that day. I was firing at the Germans.

Revd Charles Stuart, Padre, Gordon Highlanders, Banchory

You will soon get the official story in the papers. You will read of a really terrific battle in which the Gordons once again emerged victorious to cover themselves with glory. Incidentally, if you read of any story giving my name, take it with a pinch of salt. The Padre gave the story and stuck in my name.

Willie McPherson, letter, late June 1944

In fact, McPherson had organised the defence of the HQ, knocked out a machine-gun, silenced a sniper and won the Military Medal.

The last straw came when the newsreel camera folk wanted a rehearsal for a 'take'. So I said, 'On your way, brother, the war's still on out here.'

Willie McPherson, letter, late June 1944

Probably about half our time would be with Scottish regiments. They were usually quite pleased to see us, very often astonished, wondered what on earth we were supposed to be

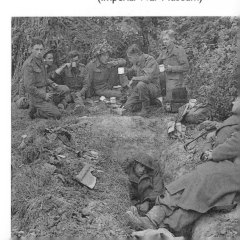

An army cameraman captured other men of the 5th/7th Gordons brewing up round a slit trench near Touffreville, 17 June 1944
(Imperial War Museum)

doing. I remember one little Scots lad saying, 'Are ye takin' photies? God, I wouldn't have your job for a pension!' And I said, 'Well, I certainly wouldn't have yours. Because you're in a slit trench all night!'

John Gordon, army film unit cameraman, Castle Douglas

I saw a fellow with a camera in his hand and I heard him say to one Jock, 'Kneel down, lad, and point your gun up the road. Look as though you're doing something.' I called him over and I said, 'They are doing something, you know, they're going into action.'

James Irvine, Gordon Highlanders, Drumoak

I remember in France, one of the officers brought a document issued from Hollywood by some of the directors who were making war films using our footage. It listed the things they were not getting – including hand-to-hand fighting and bayonet work. You can guess what sort of reaction that brought!

John Gordon

On 9 June 1944, the King's Own Scottish Borderers went into action at Cambes-en-Plaine.

This was the first time we actually got into hand-to-hand fighting with the Germans. Because by then the Hitler Jugend Panzer Division had moved down towards us. So we had to dig in pretty smartly.

George Duncan, KOSB, Edinburgh

We had to dig holes in the ground like rats. Because of the firing, you could only take a couple of shovels full and you had to duck down again. Eventually you got a trench made.

Geoffrey McCreath, KOSB, Berwick-on-Tweed

Cambes Wood was like something from the First World War. We were dug in, the wood was being constantly shelled and mortared and we were pinned down. There was a lot of small-arms fire whistling through the woods.

James Barclay, KOSB, West Kilbride

It was the first time most of us had ever seen dead bodies, except in a wild west film. Our shirts were impregnated with some kind of vermin protective thing and we didn't seem to smell, but the Germans had this rather smelly scented thing and it was odd that the German dead smelt different to ours.

'C' Company, 1st
Battalion KOSBs,
(Vic Campbell)

George Duncan

I jumped out of my trench and a shell landed beside me and blew me across the ground. I found I couldn't run and I felt some liquid running down my leg. I found I'd been wounded.

Geoffrey McCreath

We were lifting a mine with trip wires. One of my men just touched a wire – he was wounded rather badly and I got a bit in my side. That was the end of me for the moment.

George Duncan

I am told that a platoon commander on D-Day had a fortnight to live. That was his life expectancy. So I reckon I'd been pretty lucky.

Geoffrey McCreath

The Allies had planned to capture Caen on D-Day. A month later, it was still in German hands.

On 8 July we were on the high ground above Caen. The five hundred bombers, Allied bombers, came over in formation and absolutely devastated the town, plastered it, terrible bombing. The KOSB were the first infantry into Caen. The most amazing thing was that civilians began to appear from their cellars from under the rubble with bottles of wine and cider, bunches of flowers. A member of the Resistance said to me, 'If you are wounded, can I have your rifle?' So I informed him I had no intention of being wounded and I kept my rifle.

James Barclay

The worst action when I was there was at Troarn. I think the aerial bombardment of Caen had maybe knocked a bit of the life out of the Germans, but it certainly hadn't affected them at Troarn. I was one of a group of three who had contacted Germans at very close range. My friend had ordered me into an orchard to do some firing on the flank. When I got back he was dying – he had been shot in the head and the other chap was shot in the leg. He died eventually.

Vic Campbell, KOSB, Catrine

The company consisted of about 120 men. I was told that there were about nineteen or twenty men who survived a certain attack that they went into at Troarn. Of course I wasn't there, otherwise I wouldn't be speaking to you today.

Geoffrey McCreath

Geoffrey McCreath: 'pretty lucky' (Geoffrey McCreath)

By the time the third action at Monte Sanger in August took place, the battalion as I knew it had somehow died. We had lost something like **48** per cent of our original numbers.

Vic Campbell

The Germans realised that there was a danger of being cut off at Falaise, so they moved all their tanks to keep the gap open and withdraw all their troops through this corridor, no more than about five or six miles wide. The weather was good and the Air Force literally slaughtered the retreating Germans. I can still remember the smell of death over that area, both human and horses.

John Gordon

It was like going down a narrow alleyway of dead everything. We tried putting on our gas masks to stop the awful smell because it was just about the hottest time, and it really was an appalling sight.

James Irvine

Over 10,000 Germans died at Falaise and 50,000 were taken prisoner.

There were about seventy prisoners and all our Jocks started booing at them. I was furious and told them to shut up. But after the first action, the first thing a Jock would do was take out his packet of cigarettes and give the prisoner one. There was a fellow feeling between them.

James Irvine

Willie McPherson: 'I'd hate to think we couldn't last it out now' (Miss Blackhall McPherson)

Some SS men would actually spit at you. They were still arrogant, even as prisoners. But the actual German soldiers, the Wehrmacht, they were good soldiers.

John Russell

You didn't take many SS prisoners, they just fought till the finish. Any dirty trick you had to be ready for.

James Irvine

Those three were really lucky I took them instead of shooting. Just five minutes before that I saw two of our stretcher-bearers killed by a Gerry machine-gun. They were murdered in cold blood because they were not carrying weapons of any description and were wearing the Red Cross arm-bands, which could not have been mistaken at that range. I swore there and then I would never take another prisoner. My finger itched to pull the trigger, but it would have been too much like murder.

Willie McPherson, letter, 3 July 1944

Some 37,000 Allied servicemen died to liberate France, and a further 153,000 were wounded.

If I'm proud of the regiment, can you blame me? They gave so much, and through it all I have borne a charmed life. The boys marvel at my apparent lack of nerve. Some say, 'He'll get it yet.' Others refer to me as mad.

Willie McPherson, letter, August 1944

I suppose that wasn't a bad fault in war, was it? I think you've got to be a bit crazy to deal with that sort of thing.

Jimmy George

He was a real hard man. He was not scared of anything. He went forward where he should maybe have taken cover.

Bill Paterson, Gordon Highlanders, Aboyne

If they only knew how really scared I am. But if they can stick it, I can. But how, oh how, I would welcome the finish of it all. You may think I am losing heart. I'm not, but I admit I'm beginning to feel war-weary in common with the rest of the old hands. We've done so much to win this war, so much to be proud of. I'd hate to think we couldn't last it out now.

Willie McPherson, letter, August 1944

Willie McPherson's grave photographed by a family member shortly after the war (Miss Blackhall McPherson)

On 29 August 1944, at Yville-Sur-Seine, Willie McPherson was killed leading his patrol into action.

I think a sniper got him. It showed the strength of his character, the fact that he had pushed on out there on his own – almost inviting the sniper to catch him.

Revd Charles Stuart

Betty's letter to Willie – posted the day before he was killed

When I heard he'd got the Military Medal, I wrote to him, but my letter was returned unopened. He never got it. How did we hear? We got a telegram. I was in service in Aberdeen and I got leave to come home for the night because Peggy was so upset. Peggy never really got over Willie's death. She died two months later from a stroke. It was sad – very sad.

Betty Blackhall McPherson

In August Paris was liberated and by September the 51st Highland Division had reached the scene of their 1940 surrender, Saint-Valery-en-Caux.

There were quite a number of us who escaped from the Germans and came back into the Division. The Germans had left the town the day before and Monty arranged that the Highland Division should come back and we should liberate the town where our forebears had been captured. We had a lovely triumphal entry and the French civilians welcomed us with open arms. And that warm relationship with Scotland has lasted to the present day.

Derek Lang, Cameron Highlanders, Midlothian

In late September the failure of the attack at Arnhem killed hopes of a quick end to the war. After a long cold winter and other reverses, the Allies finally reached Germany in late March of 1945. A quarter of a million men, led by Commandos and the 15th Scottish and 51st Highland Division, crossed the physical and psychological barrier of the Rhine.

The German troops fought on bitterly right up to 8 May when the war ended. There were Hitler Jugend battalions and other fanatical groups fighting on till the last moment.

James Barclay

On 7 May 1945, Germany signed an unconditional surrender. In Bremerhaven in Northern Germany, German officers surrendered to the 51st Highland Division.

Out of 120 of us all called up on the same day in January 1942, I wouldn't say there were twenty of us that came through without a scratch. I was one of the very lucky ones.

Bill Cheyne, Gordon Highlanders, Newburgh

Those that were lucky enough to keep from being killed or wounded were in the thick of it all the time. We never got a break. It's a long trek from Alamein to Bremerhaven.

Sandy Grant, Gordon Highlanders, Aberdeen

CHAPTER 22

Bamboo and Barbed Wire

Many Scots spent most of the war as prisoners of the Japanese and the Germans. By the time the reformed 51st Highland Division had liberated Saint–Valery–en Caux, the first 51st had been prisoners for five years.

I hated the Germans. I was completely demoralised with the whole thing – that we were in a prison camp when we should be fighting. Particularly when we were in the 51st Highland Division – the famous 51st – and we'd made a botch of it.

Jack Hunter, Royal Artillery, Millport

We were put on the infamous cattle trucks for three days and two nights – sixty to a truck –and you were just pushed in and the door slammed shut. So we trundled along all the way to Poland. We ended up on the border of Prussia south–east of Danzig. It was very, very cold.

Donald Alan MacLean, Cameron Highlanders, Inverness

You talk about being hungry. You've had a game of golf and you think you're hungry. That's not hunger, not the hunger when your back meets your front.

Sinclair Cameron, Royal Artillery, Millport

The Germans took photographs for the PoWs to send home (Jack Hunter)

The boys would steal from each other; they would cheat, fight with each other over a crust of bread. Food was the dominating factor. That was all you thought about all day, all night – food.

Walter Kerr, Royal Artillery, Millport

There was a dirty pond in the camp. It was green with slime and that was all the water we had.

Murdo MacCuish, Cameron Highlanders, North Uist

People think you were stuck in a camp all day and did nothing. We had to work twelve hours a day. It was

LOCAL PRISONERS OF WAR IN GERMANY.

Back row:—Jack Hunter, Ian Speirs, John Fraser M'Naughton (Millport). (Millport). (Millport).
Front row:—Dougie M'Lean, James M'Laughlin, Eric Rafferty (Rothesay). (Millport). (Millport).

winter and thick snow and we had to sweep the streets and, boy, it was cold.

Walter Kerr

We went to work on the farms and that was hard labour. Every night you hoped you wouldn't wake up, but you would, and the grind started all over again.

Murdo MacCuish

Then the Red Cross parcels started coming in, and the first one was divided among five hundred. So that was a great excitement for a whole week.

Donald MacLean, Black Watch, Perth

Suddenly a shout would go up – 'The Red Cross parcels are here!' And everybody would be happy and singing. It was a link with home – especially to see Cadbury's chocolate.

David Stevenson, Royal Artillery, Millport

All our dried fruit from our parcels and sugar beet – we boiled it up with yeast. And we stayed up all night to distil it. In the morning we were kind of half–cut tasting it. But we got about 14 bottles out of it. This was for Hogmanay night. We wrapped blankets round us, bare legs, and had a dance. The English, they didn't put on a show at all. And the Germans were saying: 'Where the hell are they getting that drink?'

Bill Crossan, Cameron Highlanders, Glasgow

Jim Atkinson's PoW
pipeband, 1944
(Jim Atkinson)

We persuaded the Germans there'd be a riot if we couldn't have a party on Hogmanay or St Andrew's Night. We got musical instruments from various places, ran a pipeband and did Highland dancing. I devised one dance – the St Valery Reel – but you don't really celebrate a defeat and the name was changed to the Reel of the 51st Division.

Jim Atkinson, Argyll and Sutherland Highlanders, Alloa

Being bandsmen, we started agitating and got instruments and had terrific music. I remember the orchestra played a big concert and the commandant arrived in all his glory with his whole gang – the Iron Crosses and daggers and big jackboots – and we played Beethoven's Fifth and they thought it was great.

Donald MacLean

Walter Kerr, the boxer
(Walter Kerr)

We had a boxing team and we were taken to a hall and they'd built a real boxing ring with lights. The place was packed. There were all these German officers with their – well, they said they were their wives but I doubt it – with their fancy bits. All round, watching us boxing.

Walter Kerr

Some people decided to put on plays. Noel Coward sort of people. They made wigs out of horse–hair and cotton–wool and a lot of the young boys dressed up as girls. We learnt some Maori dances from the New Zealanders and it took us all our time to learn to be ladies and wobble our hips around.

Jim Atkinson

Jim Atkinson 'wobbling those hips' in the back row, centre
(Jim Atkinson)

A rare photograph of a PoW audience
(Walter Kerr)

This lad had a letter from his wife to say that she had had a baby to someone else. This was the second time it had happened and it upset him a lot. There was quite a number of lads got letters from home saying, 'You ran away from the Germans, so I'm running away from you.'

David Stevenson

You missed your home. I was sent golf shoes, and the mud from the Millport golf course was in the treads. I sat taking this mud out and put

it in a matchbox. The men thought I was mad. But I took it back home and put it back where it came from.

Sinclair Cameron

If anyone escaped it would be RAF people because they had more knowledge of navigation. The ordinary Jock like myself, I was in Germany somewhere, but I could have been in Timbuktu.

Donald MacLean

I remember one day in the winter when it was bitterly cold and the commandant opened the camp gates. He said, 'Anyone who wants to can go.' And it was a frozen wasteland outside, stretching to the horizon. Twenty degrees below and there were wolves in the woods. Further along, they told us, there were bears. So no one took him up on that.

Walter Kerr

The first year was so bad that I went to bed at night and prayed that I wouldn't wake up in the morning. I reached the depths. But funny enough, as you went on you got stronger. And at the end we felt superior to the Germans.

Jack Hunter

One German guard used to call us *kluger* – 'fly men'. He regarded us as very devious. We were always up to something. The aim was to survive, to forage, to ferret out. I was pretty good at it myself.

Donald Alan MacLean

We always thought we'd win in the end. It was a nasty thing not to think that. Because some of them went a wee bit wrong in the head. Barbed–wire fever we called it. But we're all made different.

Sinclair Cameron

For Argylls and Gordons captured by the Japanese at the fall of Singapore, there were no camp concerts, Red Cross parcels or letters from home.

Everyone was pretty apprehensive because the Japanese did not belong to the Geneva Convention and they didn't normally take prisoners. But I suppose there were so many of us and we were going to be useful to them as a labour force. They despised us – as they do an enemy who surrenders. For the Japanese, to die in battle is the biggest honour there is.

Moubray Burnett, Gordon Highlanders, New Machar

We were told not to look at the Japanese officer because we were a degraded people. He referred to us as the tattered remnants of a decadent race.

Archie Black, Gordon Highlanders, Gretna

We were asked to sign a petition that we wouldn't escape and, of course, in the army you're not permitted to do that. So we were all squeezed into this barracks at Selarang. It was called 'The Squeeze'.

Iain McKenzie, Gordon Highlanders, Stirling

There were 18,000 people in a square fit for 300 men. We held out for a while, but diphtheria, dysentery and malaria broke out.

Tom McGregor, Argyll and Sutherland Highlanders, Falkirk

We were forced to sign this bit of paper which didn't mean anything. Once you were up in Thailand there was no possibility of escape. You were a white face and how many miles of jungle would you have to get through to get to India?

Moubray Burnett

The Allied PoWs were to become slave labour, laying 258 miles of track on the Thai–Burma railway.

'The Squeeze' at Selarang, 1942 (Archie Black)

The Death Railway. I was on that from the start to the finish. The death rate was absolutely ridiculous and scandalous — the numbers that died in Japanese hands in three years and seven months.

Jockie Bell, Argyll and Sutherland Highlanders, Renfrew

We were working about twelve hours a day, and even though you were sick you were carried out on stretchers to help build the embankments.

Finlay MacLachlan, Argyll and Sutherland Highlanders, High Bonnybridge

In the Gordons, we were all used to working on the land. But we felt sorry for the Englishmen. They found it very hard.

Norman Catto, Gordon Highlanders, Scone

It's hard to fathom now, but we came home from working parties in the pouring rain with bare feet and wearing a loin cloth. And we used to sing, 'She'll be coming round the mountain when she comes'. The Japs loved that, but they must have thought we were crazy. We'd done a horrible day's work out in the rain for a bowl of rice. And you're marching back singing at the top of your voice to keep your spirits up.

Jockie Bell

I was responsible for liaising with the Japanese officer, who, fortunately, had been an undergraduate at Cambridge. He was quite a reasonable character to deal with. But I had a very difficult sergeant who armed himself with a spear. His main hobby in the evening was to get me to stand to attention and lunge at me with this spear, saying, 'Burnetto, go paradiso.' That was his main amusement. But it wasn't mine.

Moubray Burnett

They picked on people for nothing. If a man collapsed they beat him and you had to carry the body back and perhaps he died through the night. They were definitely savages, these people.

Jockie Bell

The sergeant came along to where we were working and he said we weren't hitting the rock at the right angle. So he took the chisel out of the bloke's hands and put it in at the angle he wanted. There were two Gordons and one had the hammer and he was shaking like a leaf. He swung at the chisel and missed it, hitting the sergeant on the hand. He was most annoyed and took the hammer and thumped it right across his skull and split it open.

Iain McKenzie

Death Railway – built at a rate of one life per metre of track
(Archie Black)

Three escaped one night and were away for three days. They were brought back and beheaded in front of us. That was a lesson to us. It was impossible to get away – and where could we go? It was jungle, jungle, jungle.

Norman Catto

I used to run about with ulcers on my feet. You used to go down to the river and put your feet in and the fish would come and pick off all the dead bits.

Finlay MacLachlan

The orderlies put maggots on to clean out the wounds. I was lucky. A great many lost their legs.

Norman Catto

The medical officers were fantastic. They were performing operations with nothing. Using razor blades, any old thing, amputating legs with no anaesthetic.

Duncan Ferguson, Argyll and Sutherland Highlanders, Falkirk

When cholera struck I was really scared. You didn't know who it was going to affect. You were speaking to a chap before you fell asleep and you woke up in the morning and he was dead. There were a lot of deaths from cholera and we burned all the bodies.

Norman Catto

I remember being on the burning party. We had to build a fire of dry bamboo sticks, put the body wrapped in sacks on top and set fire to it. It was a really horrible experience for a young fellow like myself.

Iain McKenzie

I think a lot of them lost heart. They didn't all die of disease in my opinion. A lot of them just lay down and gave up. I remember talking to two young English boys and they were saying 'We'll never get out of this. What's the use?' They were both dead within a fortnight.

Finlay MacLachlan

I saw two or three dead bodies floating down the river. People that had just given up. I fell in and couldn't get up the bank. It was slippery with mud. I lay back and said 'What's the use?' and was quite prepared to go. Then I heard my mother's voice, clear as anything, saying, 'Come on, Norman, you'll get home.'

Norman Catto

'Come on, Norman...'
Mrs Catto's photograph
of her son
(Norman Catto)

Of the 50,000 British troops captured at Singapore, 12,000 died in the Japanese camps.

For the Highland Division, scattered in camps on the Eastern Front in Europe, it was the final march to freedom that took the greatest toll.

When the Russian offensive broke on 20 January 1945, they marched us like cattle in a westerly direction. Our march to Poland, let me be quite blunt about it, simply paled into insignificance compared with the Baltic march. That was the test of survival.

Donald Alan MacLean

A German came running in and he said, 'The Russians are very close. You know the kind of war we're fighting. If you want to go out to the Russians, you'll be shot because they won't recognise any uniform. What we're going to do is go on the march.' And I thought, 'Oh no, not again.'

Walter Kerr

We marched all day and at night were put into a field and some of them were able to light fires. But it dawned on me that if you sat about you were going to freeze. So I just kept moving around all night long – didn't sleep. And sure enough, in the morning, daylight came and the boys were laying there dead, frozen.

Jack Hunter

We were forever pulling boys up off the ground and slapping their faces and saying, 'Wake up. Keep going.' Because once you'd fallen asleep, you'd had it.

Walter Kerr

Every time we bumped into the Russians they gave us a beating up and tried to take our boots off us. The result was, when we saw Russians coming, we hid in the snow.

Jack Hunter

We walked down the autobahn from Hamburg to Berlin. The American planes used to come over and have a bit of fun, machine–gunning us.

Murdo MacCuish

British planes come over firing rockets. They killed eighty prisoners and six Germans.

Sinclair Cameron

Then one day the American tanks broke through and that was us liberated. The guards were taken prisoner. The bad guards took off because they knew they would be for it. And there were only decent guards with us that day. The Americans said, 'Do you want to get your own back? Because tomorrow it will be law and order.' But we never touched anyone; we knew what it was like to be taken prisoner.

Murdo MacCuish

The 15th Scottish liberated us on this farm. And the Germans all threw their rifles away. Nobody was to blame for the war, you see.

Sinclair Cameron

We took over this house owned by a middle–aged couple and – all's fair in love and war – we chucked them down the cellar. They were only too happy to be there. We raided the old man's chest and had a bath for the first time in five years.

Donald Alan MacLean

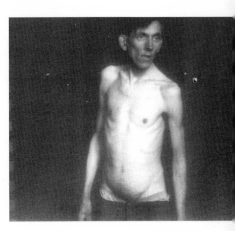

We landed in England and kissed the ground. We couldn't eat a bite. We weren't used to white bread. It was all that black bread – green-moulded. That's what we were used to. But that was us, on the way back home to Bonnie Scotland.

Bill Crossan

A rare newsreel shot of a survivor of the 'atrocity known as the Baltic trek' (British Movietone News)

Some treated us as dirt because we were prisoners. I filled in a form to claim campaign medals and one of the officers tore it up. He said, 'You're not entitled to medals. You were a prisoner-of-war.' It was such a waste of time. But an experience – an experience I could have done well without.

Jack Hunter

On 6 August 1945, an atomic bomb was dropped on Hiroshima, followed three days later by another on Nagasaki. On 14 August, Japan agreed to unconditional surrender.

We got up one morning and there was no working party, no roll call. Four chaps went out on a scouting party and the natives told them, 'The war is finished. The Japanese all go.' We never saw another hide nor hair of a Jap.

Duncan Ferguson

We were always worried that the Japanese would massacre us. We were lined up and marched through a little gate. But there was an Australian at

the other side and he shook our hands and said, 'It's all over.'

Archie Black

We were going to do all sorts of things to the Japanese. We were going to murder the lot of them. But when it came to it, they kept to themselves and we kept to ourselves.

Norman Catto

Prisoners of the Japanese, 1945 (Archie Black)

I've never seen so many people crying. All the pent–up emotions broke. And they were all hard men who had fought the Japs and come back. Everything seemed to release all at once.

Finlay MacLachlan

You had to go to the cookhouse and the queue just kept going round and round. It was never–ending. The cook said, 'Where the hell are they all coming from?' It was just the same boys going round and round, eating. You knew it would make you sick, but you just couldn't stop eating.

Duncan Ferguson

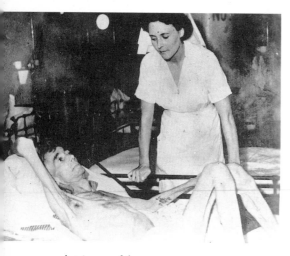

I think they're brutal, cruel, wicked people. I know some people do, but I can never forgive them for what people suffered under them.

Moubray Burnett

I hate them. I've got a wee pal, he's forgiven them. He's a true Christian. But me, I'll never forgive them, never.

Duncan Ferguson

A prisoner of the Japanese on his way home (Archie Black)

The prisoners that were there are very close to one another. We can actually say 'I love you' without any offence being taken. Only we really know what we've been through.

Tom McGregor

CHAPTER 23

Winning the Peace?

VE Day was celebrated on 8 May 1945.

To say that everybody went out onto the street and danced is wrong. There were some mothers who cried, because they were waiting for sons who would never come home.

Bella Keyzer, Dundee

There was tremendous rejoicing but it was muted because the Japanese had still to be beaten and I was then fifteen, rising sixteen, and I thought, 'This war's only got to be on for another two years. And you're going to find out about it the hard way.'

Bob Crampsey, Glasgow

Victory bonfire in a Glasgow street (*Herald/Times*)

The Japanese guards began to drink sake and we knew their morale had gone. Someone said, 'They've dropped a horrible bomb.'

Drummond Hunter, PoW Hong Kong, Edinburgh

There we were training again for the invasion of Japan. It would have been a murderous adventure. It would have cost a million men. Then who I call Saint Harry Truman dropped the bomb.

George Duncan, King's Own Scottish Borderers, Edinburgh

Nothing came as more of a relief as the dropping of the atomic bomb and even more joy when the second one dropped on Nagasaki. Anyone who had been to Burma would know that anything was preferable to having to go another day in those conditions.

Archie Toppin, Indian Army, Glasgow

Even if these bombs did hasten the end of the war, I would question whether you are entitled to do so by committing a war crime.

Drummond Hunter

VJ Day was celebrated on 14 August 1945.

My own town seemed a terribly small place after I got back. Although it is great to come back to life again, it is also a very painful process.

Drummond Hunter

I just sat at the fire and never said anything. It took a long, long while to come round. We just didn't talk and I gather that was the same with most of the other boys. Nobody wanted to talk. We just sat there.

Walter Kerr, PoW Germany, Millport

My brother was killed at El Alamein. So when I met my mother in Glasgow, she said, 'Did you know about the boys?' There were another two I didn't know anything about. So I lost three brothers during the war and one was wounded. That was my homecoming.

Finlay MacLachlan, PoW Burma, High Bonnybridge

I met my son when I came home. The wife was expecting when I went away and he was nearly five by then.

Jockie Bell, PoW Burma, Renfrew

Four MacLachlan brothers from Stirlingshire were pipers in the Argylls. Finlay (third) was a prisoner of the Japanese, Malcolm (first) and Ian (second) were killed in the same week in North Africa piping their regiment into action, and Kenneth (fourth) was disabled by shrapnel (Finlay MacLachlan)

Life back in Civvy Street was complicated for everybody.

Jockie Bell and his wife photographed before he embarked for Singapore (Jockie Bell)

The children were quite funny about it. They were hanging onto my skirt and saying, 'Who's this man?' They weren't too sure about him. So that was a bit of an upset, but otherwise it was smashing.

Bette Stivens, Edinburgh

One of the neighbour's boys came to the door in the early morning shouting, 'Margaret! Here's John.' 'Aye,' I said, 'that'll be right.' He'd been away for years. And do you know, it was! When you look back you wonder how you got through these days. Love's a great thing!

Margaret Docherty, Glasgow

I remember saying to my father long after I had married, 'What would have happened to me if there hadn't been a war?' And he said, 'You'd have stayed at home and looked after your mother.' Can you imagine? So thanks to the war I joined the Wrens and got away. I liked mother, but I didn't want to be a domestic slave for the rest of my life.

Marjorie Herd, Thornton, Fife

I was looking forward but I was scared. How was I going to get on in civvy life again? Would I go back to the same job? I was comfortable in the WAAF.

Irene Milne, Edinburgh

You were supposed to come back to the job you had before you went in. You could have been an office boy or a junior clerk and if you were twenty-six or twenty-seven, you didn't want to do this. And they didn't want you either.

Joyce Anderson, Orkney

I couldn't find a chair to sit on. They hadn't enough chairs. I'm not a man that wants a lot out of life, but I thought this is not making me the most welcome hero. So I stayed there for about five days and still couldn't find a chair, and quit and went back to work in Hong Kong.

Harry Sullivan, Commando, Macclesfield

My brother was in the Commandos and I think he wasn't happy to be in the glen again. He wanted to be where things were moving because he'd seen so much of the world.

Jean Mitchell, Blairgowrie

My nineteenth birthday was spent in Fort George when I was first called up. My twentieth birthday was spent on the Anzio beachhead, and my

twenty-first birthday was spent in a prisoner-of-war camp.

Norman Smith, Isle of Lewis

These six years felt like twenty years. For a long while I could place exactly where I was. I could tell you that on 3 March '41 we were up in Norway at Lofoten. On 19 August '42 we were in Dieppe. Whereas, after the war it was difficult to separate 1963 from 1964 – you had to remember where you went on holiday.

Bill Boucher-Myers, Troon

The war left me a more jumpy person. Because I found with all the action, for long after I'd come home, if a gate banged I was ready to flatten out on my face. I never really got over it.

John Russell, Dundee

Bill Boucher-Myers discusses casualty figures with Lord Lovat on the Commandos' return from the Dieppe raid (Bill Boucher-Myers)

I suppose I was a nervous young man and I'm still bothered with nerves. But I just have to get on with living and do the best I can. But it still bothers me.

Geoffrey McCreath, Berwick-on-Tweed

I feel I have been living on borrowed time since I was twenty years of age. The casualties out of a battalion strength of 800 were 600 killed and wounded.

James Barclay, West Kilbride

Of all my school friends, not one of them was alive. I counted on my school memorial ninety-eight people of my own age who were killed during the war. They were just the right age, you see.

Peter Wild, Kelso

Why we are still left is not a question for us to answer. It is in the fore-ordained providence of an Almighty God and that is why we are here.

Norman Smith

I don't think I was changed by the war experience. I was changed by losing a leg. There's no question that a major disability gives you a different view on life.

Denis Forman, Moffat

It's made me very cynical. But that's common with most servicepeople. We're probably great believers in sod's law, because we've seen so much of it.

Vic Campbell, Catrine

In prison camp, people used to say, 'Wait till we get back to normal.' But gradually, people began to say, 'There will be no normal. The world is never going to be the same again.'

Drummond Hunter

The class system seemed weaker at the end of the war than it had been at the beginning when young communist, Stuart Hood, became an officer.

The officers usually referred to the men as the 'sweaty Jocks'. That was how they saw them – as a different species. And indeed they were, socially and psychologically.

Stuart Hood, Edzell

One of four children from a room-and-kitchen in Glasgow's Maryhill, Archie Toppin found himself in an officer training unit.

There was an element of class, but it was a lower definition of class. I was a university student. If I had gone up there as a brickie, I don't know what the attitude would have been to me. One wonders. All I know is that when I became an officer I didn't meet many brickies.

Archie Toppin

There were a lot more working-class people getting commissions. The other thing was that the war was a great big sacrifice, so it had to be a sacrifice for something worth while – for the new sunlit society away from the depression of the 1930s.

Cliff Hanley, Glasgow

I think this permeated not only the ranks, but many of the officers as well. And what we could call the 'temporary gentlemen' like myself, who'd

FROM TOP TO BOTTOM:
Living on borrowed time: KOSB James Barclay
Not one schoolfriend left alive: Naval Lieutenant Peter Wild
Foreordained providence: Reconnaissance Corps soldier Norman Smith
Never the same again: Royal Scots officer, Drummond Hunter, before his capture by the Japanese

Archie Toppin
(back row, left) in the
Officers' Training Unit –
he didn't meet many
brickies
(Archie Toppin)

been taken on for the duration. We were fighting for something quite specific.

Stuart Hood

The lads weren't going away for five years, fighting and coming back to the same conditions. They weren't going to have it. They started making demands.

Agnes McLean, Glasgow

In Cairo there were a large number of people who were, roughly speaking, on the left – and they set up a debating society which developed into a parliament with a government and opposition. The government was also to the left and they passed unanimously that all sorts of institutions should be nationalised. We were closed down by the authorities because they felt it had got out of hand.

Stuart Hood

There was a bit of political education going on, officially, in the army. You don't normally think of armies, particularly in the middle of fighting a war, indulging in this kind of thing. So you could say it was very enlightened, because the natural tendency of these discussions was to promote a view critical of the sort of society that existed before the war.

Paul Scott, Edinburgh

By the time we came to 1943 it was absolutely clear that the Allies were winning on all fronts and were bound to win the war. It got really hot then: what kind of country are we going to have after the war?

Robert Grieve, town planner, Glasgow

A report written by Liberal economist Sir William Beveridge after the victory at Alamein identified five old enemies to be defeated along with the Germans: Want, Disease, Ignorance, Squalor and Idleness. Churchill banned the report from being discussed in the army's current affairs classes, but it was a best-seller.

I was in a prisoner-of-war camp when the Beveridge Report came out. Somebody had a copy sent to them and the excitement that this caused was quite marked, and there were big discussions and debates about why we had been fighting. It always seemed clear to me that the army, by and large, was going to vote left.

Stuart Hood

I wonder if it's possible to get across to you the feeling in 1945? The feeling of elation among people of my age wasn't so much about having won a war. It was that there was a capability of a new start and the feeling among ordinary men, in what we called the lower deck, was that – unquestionably – there would be a change in British government at the next election. But this wasn't the feeling that one got from one's officers.

Ian MacInnes, Orkney

They just had a one-track mind: King and Empire, King and Empire. And possibly public school, Eton, Oxford and Cambridge – that sort of thing.

Archie Toppin

Some of the senior officers were saying, 'The war's not going to finish. Because after we've finished with this lot, we're just going to go on against the Russians. So you'll probably be in for another five years.' This was the attitude of some of them.

Ian MacInnes

I could understand the men because they wanted to get back to their loved ones, and their loved ones were telling them, 'You'd better vote Labour because they'll bring you back. Mr Churchill has other things in store for the British Empire.' So these lads quite rightly went into the polling booths and put their cross for Labour.

Bill Boucher-Myers

One didn't get any localised type of election address. It would have been impossible for the member standing for Maryhill to send an election address out to me in the Burmese jungle.

Archie Toppin

Mr Churchill's reception was spectacular on his election tour and it seems to be agreed that Scotland outdid even England. In Edinburgh, he paid tribute to the great part Scotland played in winning the war – to its famous fighting divisions, its sailors and airmen, and the men and women of the factories and coal-mines. The scene in Glasgow was on the same grand scale as Edinburgh. In fact, Scotland did Mr Churchill proud! By the time these pictures appear in the cinema, the country will have gone to the polls and the fate of Mr Churchill's government will be in the bag.

***Mr Churchill in Scotland*, British Movietone News, June 1945**

I heard him speaking at that time in Blythswood Square in Glasgow. He was up on a balcony giving it big licks – a great speech. We all loved him. We all

Ian MacInnes: 'a feeling of elation'
(Ian MacInnes)

thought he was a great man and we all hoped that his regime would *not* continue into the peace. I think it was pretty universal.

Robert Grieve

On 26 July 1945, the General Election result was a Labour landslide.

I was a bit shattered — as a Conservative. I remember in the ward-room when we got the result some people said, 'Well, that's it. We've had it.'

Peter Wild

The upper classes had shifted around and taken up strong positions in the new order. I don't think they gave away an inch actually. They were quite willing to use people like myself who had certain skills. I think it was quite clear at the end of the war that they were going to need some of us, but not many of us, and these people would have to be very carefully chosen.

Stuart Hood

We were going to move forward into this great socialist Utopia. We finally came down with a bump, of course. What they didn't do was tackle the state machine. They were still tightly in control: the whole state machine, the civil service, the forces, the chiefs of staff, the employers, the big boys. They were all firmly in control.

Agnes McLean

We did feel it was to be a new world, a better world, and of course in a way it was. Everybody was ready for change. But it was at the far end of the tunnel — and we never got there.

Naomi Mitchison, Carradale

Naomi Mitchison doesn't just speak with hindsight. Throughout the war, she kept a daily diary running to a million words for the Mass Observation Organisation. Fifty years ago, she closed her diary with the words:

Well, here is the end of the war and the end of this diary . . . I know we are going to have hell trying to work the peace, trying to give people a worth-while-ness in their peacetime lives comparable with the worth-while-ness of working together during the war. We shall probably fail.

Naomi Mitchison's diary, 12 August 1945

Naomi Mitchison in Carradale, Mull of Kintyre, where she lived for most of the war (Naomi Mitchison)

BIBLIOGRAPHICAL BACKGROUND

A full bibliography of all books on the Second World War would be a mad endeavour and a long book in itself. But when you turn to Scotland in particular, there is much less published material to choose from. All we wish to do here is present some examples of publications and sources we found useful to help us keep to the straight and narrow of historical fact. Even compiling this list confirms the importance of recording these *Scotland's War* memories, with all the flaws of hindsight. Without them, there would be no personal record of many areas of Scottish experience. Memoirs such as Sir Derek Lang's *Return to St Valery* (London 1974) or Sir Denis Forman's *To Reason Why* (London 1991) are usually written by the officers and not by the men. Local pictorial accounts such as Paul Harris's *Glasgow at War* (Manchester 1986) and *Aberdeen at War* (Manchester 1987) only give an impression of what minutiae of home front life newspapers chose to cover – or what the official censor allowed to slip through the net. The censor at *The Scotsman* was apparently particularly enthusiastic about smashing glass plate negatives of aspects of Edinburgh life which could prove useful to Hitler!

Our bible was inevitably *The People's War* by Angus Calder (London 1969). It is rare to find a book of such comprehensive range and complexity which is also witty and alive to human quirks. There is not a great deal of detail in it about Scotland, but Calder does touch on the Highland Division, Tom Johnston, Scottish Nationalism and other issues. His analysis of such complicated issues as rationing apply Britain-wide, so we have chosen not to explain how the system worked – merely how it affected some Scots from farmer to grocer to shopper to eater. An important source for a sense of the views, hopes and fears of the public in wartime – and used throughout *The People's War* – is the Mass-Observation Archive based as the University of Sussex at Brighton. M-O was founded in 1937 to study life in Britain through volunteer 'observers' and in 1940 began to study morale in everyday life and industry for the Ministry of Information. M-O volunteers throughout Britain were asked to keep diaries and one of the most complete is that kept by Naomi Mitchison, mainly in Carradale in the Mull of Kintyre, and later published as *Among You Taking Notes* (London 1985, edited by Dorothy Sheridan). It is a vivid, though untypical, record of the experiences and emotions of one politically-aware Scot in wartime. But, perhaps because of its London base, M-O did not cover Scotland well either geographically or socially. The richest material comes from early 1941 when two English non-volunteer observers investigated 'morale in Clydeside'. We have only been able to quote briefly from these fascinating reports made before and during the Clydebank Blitz, but they paint a remarkable picture of life in the West of Scotland, complete with dance halls and even an Indian restaurant. If only Scotland was more widely covered by Scottish M-O volunteers. One of the Clydeside observers comments: 'All the unconscious antagonisms which a report on any place is likely to engender from those living *in* the place may be uncomfortably increased when it is an Englishman writing about Scots!'

We have included only a brief extract in this book from our film about Tom Johnston, *The Man from Kirkintilloch*, but there is a range of material on this fascinating man, whose career is still the subject of lively debate. His own view is in *Memories* (London 1952) and there is interesting analysis of his political background in *Tom Johnston* by Graham Walker (Manchester 1988) and *Forward! Labour Politics in Scotland 1888–1988* edited by Ian Donnachie, Christopher Harvie and Ian S. Wood (Edinburgh 1989). For the story of the internment of enemy aliens, we relied on *Collar the Lot!* by Peter and Leni Gillman (London 1980) and a contemporary campaigning book, *The Internment of Aliens* by François Lafitte (London 1940).

To avoid drowning in the worldwide sweep of the armed conflict, we clung to *The World at War* by Mark Arnold-Foster (London 1973) which was written to accompany the Thames TV series. There are many books on each campaign of Scottish interest, and there are several regimental and divisional histories – for example of the 51st Highland Division, 52nd Lowland Division and the 15th Scottish Division. The Saint Valery story has generally been neglected by British military historians in favour of Dunkirk. A recent publication, *Churchill's Sacrifice of the Highland Division* by Saul David (London 1994), has renewed the controversy over whether the Division was deliberately sacrificed. We tend to feel that the 'sacrifice' argument and the strategy surrounding the surrender have eclipsed the experiences and views of the men, especially in the PoW camps and on the Baltic trek.